Juz' 'Amma

The Qur'an Code

A Study & Explanation of Themes from the Qur'an

Hamzah Abdul-Malik

THE QUR'AN CODE

IMAM GHAZALI PUBLISHING
USA – Malaysia – UK
info@imamghazali.co
www.imamghazali.co

ISBN: 978-1-966329-82-4 (HARDBACK) | 978-1-966329-88-6 (PAPERBACK)

First Edition

10 9 8 7 6 5 4 3 2 1

Contents

Publisher's Introduction IX

Sūrah al-Naba' 1

The Main Theme: Preparing for the Hereafter 1
The Context: The Doubts of the Quraysh 1
The Relationship with the Previous Sūrahs.. 2
Thematic Explanation of the Sūrah 4

Sūrah al-Nāziʿāt.. 8

The Main Theme: Dispelling Self-Delusion... 8
The Context: When will the Day Come? 9
The Relationship with Sūrah al-Naba'.. 10
Thematic Explanation of the Sūrah 11

Sūrah ʿAbasa 16

Main Theme 16
The Context: Who Benefits from Guidance?.. 17
Relationship with Sūrah al-Nāziʿāt 20
The Thematic Explanation of the Sūrah.. 20

Sūrah al-Takwīr..25

The Main Theme 25
The Context: Who is in Control?.. 26
The Relationship with Sūrah ʿAbasa 26
Thematic Explanation of the Sūrah 27

Sūrah al-Infiṭār 31
The Main Theme 31
The Context: The Delusion of Mercy 32
The Relationship with Sūrah al-Takwīr 33
Thematic Explanation of the Sūrah 34

Sūrah al-Muṭaffifīn 37
The Main Theme 37
The Context: Petty Crimes with Major Consequences 38
The Relationship with Sūrah al-Infiṭār 39
Thematic Explanation of the Sūrah 40

Sūrah al-Inshiqāq 43
The Main Theme 43
The Context: The Pursuit of Happiness 43
The Relationship With Sūrah al-Muṭaffifīn 44
Thematic Explanation of the Sūrah 45

Sūrah al-Burūj 48
The Main Theme 48
The Context: The Arc of Justice 49
The Relationship with Sūrah al-Inshiqāq 50
Thematic Explanation of the Sūrah 50

Sūrah al-Ṭāriq 53
The Main Theme 53
The Context: A Wake Up Call 53
Relationship with Sūrah al-Burūj 54
Thematic Explanation of the Sūrah 55

Sūrah al-Aʿlā 57
The Main Theme 57
The Context: Establishing the Legacy of Ibrāhīm عليه السلام 58
The Relationship with Sūrah al-Ṭāriq 59
Thematic Explanation of the Sūrah 60

Sūrah al-Ghāshiyah 63
The Main Theme 63
The Context: Providing Perspective 63
The Relationship with Sūrah al-Aʿlā 64
Thematic Explanation of the Sūrah 64

Sūrah al-Fajr 67
The Main Theme 67
The Context: The Reality of Wealth 67
The Relationship with Sūrah al-Ghāshiyah 68
Thematic Explanation of the Sūrah 69

Sūrah al-Balad 73
The Main Theme 73
The Context: Reframing Difficulty 73
The Relationship with Sūrah al-Fajr 74
Thematic Explanation of the Sūrah 75

Sūrah al-Shams 77
The Main Theme 77
Context: A Clear Example for the Quraysh 77
The Relationship with Sūrah al-Balad 78
Thematic Explanation of the Sūrah 79

Sūrah al-Layl 81
The Main Theme 81
The Context: Sincerity is Key 81
The Relationship with Sūrah al-Shams 82
Thematic Explanation of the Sūrah 83

Sūrah al-Ḍuḥā 85
The Main Theme 85
The Context: Success Comes With Time 86
The Relationship with Sūrah al-Layl 86
Thematic Explanation of the Sūrah 87

Sūrah al-Sharḥ 89
The Main Theme, Context, & Relationship with Sūrah al-Ḍuḥā 89
Thematic Explanation of the Sūrah 89

Sūrah al-Tīn 91
The Main Theme 91
The Context: From a Blessing to a Curse 91
The Relationship with Sūrah al-Sharḥ 91
Thematic Explanation of the Sūrah 92

Sūrah al-ʿAlaq 94
Main Theme 94
The Context: The Beginning of Prophethood 95
The Relationship with Sūrah al-Tīn 97
Thematic Explanation of the Sūrah 97

Sūrah al-Qadr 100
The Main Theme 100
The Context: Exponential Blessings 100
The Relationship with Sūrah al-ʿAlaq 101
Thematic Explanation of the Sūrah 102

Sūrah al-Bayyinah 105
The Main Theme & The Context 105
The Relationship With Sūrah al-Qadr 106
Thematic Explanation of the Sūrah 106

Sūrah al-Zalzalah 108
The Main Theme & The Context 108
The Relationship with Sūrah al-Bayyinah 109
Thematic Explanation of the Sūrah 109

Sūrah al-ʿĀdiyāt 111
The Main Theme & The Context 111
The Relationship with Sūrah al-Zalzalah 112
Thematic Explanation of the Sūrah 112

Sūrah al-Qāriʿah 114
The Main Theme, Context, & Relationship with Sūrah al-ʿĀdiyāt .. 114
Thematic Explanation of the Sūrah 114

Sūrah al-Takāthur 116
The Main Theme & The Context 116
The Relationship with Sūrah al-Qāriʿah 117
Thematic Explanation of the Sūrah 117

Sūrah al-ʿAṣr 119
The Theme, Context, & Relationship with Sūrah al-Takāthur 119
Thematic Explanation of the Sūrah 119

Sūrah al-Humazah 121
The Main Theme & The Context 121
The Relationship with Sūrah al-ʿAṣr 121
Thematic Explanation of the Sūrah 122

Sūrah al-Fīl 123
The Theme, Context, & Relationship with Sūrah al-Humazah 123
Thematic Explanation of the Sūrah 124

Sūrah Quraysh 126
The Theme, The Context, & The Relationship with Sūrah al-Fīl 126
Thematic Explanation of the Sūrah 127

Sūrah al-Māʿūn 128
The Main Theme, Context, & Relationship with Sūrah Quraysh 128
Thematic Explanation of the Sūrah 129

Sūrah al-Kawthar 130
The Main Theme 130
The Context 130
The Relationship with al-Māʿūn 131
Thematic Explanation of the Sūrah 132

Sūrah al-Kāfirūn 133
The Main Theme 133

The Context 133
The Relationship with Sūrah al-Kawthar 134
Thematic Explanation of the Sūrah 135

Sūrah al-Naṣr 137
The Main Theme & The Context 137
The Relationship with Sūrah al-Kāfirūn 138
Thematic Explanation of the Sūrah 138

Sūrah al-Masad 140
The Main Theme, Context, and Relationship with Sūrah al-Naṣr .. 140
Thematic Explanation of the Sūrah 141

Sūrah al-Ikhlāṣ 143
Main Theme & The Context 143
The Relationship with Sūrah al-Masad 144
Thematic Explanation of the Sūrah 144

Sūrahs al-Falaq & al-Nās 147
The Main Theme, Context, & Relationship with Sūrah al-Ikhlāṣ 147
Thematic Explanation of the Sūrah 148

Publisher's Introduction

In the name of Allah, the Most Merciful, the Compassionate

All praise and gratitude is for Allah, our most generous and merciful benefactor. He endlessly bestows His divine grace upon us and has distinguished us by selecting us to be from the *ummah* of our master Muhammad ﷺ.

I bear witness that there is none worthy of worship except Allah, and that our master Muhammad ﷺ is His last and final Messenger.

O Allah, send prayers upon our master Muhammad, the opener of what was closed, the seal of what had preceded, the helper of the truth by the Truth, and the guide to Your straight path. May Allah send prayers upon his family according to his greatness and magnificent rank.

ذَلِكَ الْكِتَابُ لَا رَيْبَ فِيهِ هُدًى لِلْمُتَّقِينَ

This is the Book about which there is no doubt, a guidance for those conscious of Allah. (*al-Baqarah*, 2)

When we published *The Endless Banquet*, we knew it was something special. We had seen how the modern world's relentless distractions made it increasingly difficult for Muslims to establish a meaningful relationship with the Qur'an. We understood the struggle of wanting to connect more deeply with the Book of Allah, but feeling overwhelmed by its vastness, unsure where to begin, or uncertain about how to apply its teachings to daily life. *The Endless Banquet* was Shaykh Hamzah Abdul-Malik's contribution to this challenge—a guide that welcomed readers into the world of the Qur'an with clarity, depth, and an appreciation of its timeless wisdom.

The response was beyond what we had anticipated. Thousands of readers from all walks of life reached out to us, sharing how *The Endless*

Banquet had transformed their Ramadan experience and, in many cases, their relationship with the Qur'an itself. Some had read the Qur'an for years but found themselves seeing it in a new light. Others had struggled to connect with its meanings and now felt an unbreakable bond with its words. Many told us that the book had given them a sense of companionship with the Qur'an, making it a daily presence in their lives rather than a text reserved for occasional recitation. This was what we had hoped for: a revival of love for the Qur'an, a rekindling of the soul's yearning for its guidance.

And yet, as transformative as *The Endless Banquet* was, it was only the beginning of the journey. The book laid the foundation for engagement with the Qur'an, but the hunger for deeper understanding remained. The question we heard most often from readers was: *How do I go further? How do I unlock the deeper meanings of the Qur'an?*

That question has led us to *The Qur'an Code* by Shaykh Hamzah Abdul-Malik.

* * *

The Qur'an Code is a book about unlocking the Qur'an's deeper meanings, about moving beyond surface-level reading into a realm where every word resonates with purpose and insight. The author, Shaykh Hamzah Abdul-Malik, is uniquely qualified for this task. With years of rigorous study under some of the most esteemed scholars of our time, he brings a rare combination of scholarly depth and accessibility. He understands not only the intricacies of Qur'anic language, structure, and composition but also the struggles of the modern Muslim.

At its core, *The Qur'an Code* is a key—a key to approaching the Qur'an with a sense of clarity, coherence, and profound appreciation for its literary and linguistic brilliance. Shaykh Hamzah Abdul-Malik takes readers on a journey through the patterns, themes, and structural intricacies of the Qur'an, showing how nothing in the Book of Allah is arbitrary. Every word choice, every shift in address, every repeated phrase has a function and a meaning that enriches our understanding of the message. The Qur'an is not a collection of disconnected verses but a unified whole, designed with divine precision to guide, instruct, and illuminate.

The Qur'an Code is not merely an academic exercise; it is a spiritual experience. It opens the doors to seeing the Qur'an as it was meant to be seen—not just as a sacred text, but as a conversation, a dialogue between the Creator and His creation. The Qur'an is addressing *you*, and *The Qur'an Code* helps you hear that message more clearly.

* * *

If you have ever read the Qur'an and felt that there was something deeper you were not quite grasping, this book is for you.

If you have wondered about the intricate symmetry of certain surahs, the wisdom behind the placement of certain ayat, or the significance of repeated phrases, this book is for you.

If you have ever wanted to study the Qur'an more seriously but felt intimidated by complex linguistic discussions or classical tafsir, this book is for you.

The Qur'an is for everyone, and so is *The Qur'an Code*. Whether you are a student of knowledge or someone taking their first steps in understanding the deeper beauty of the Qur'an, Shaykh Hamzah Abdul-Malik's work provides an engaging, thoughtful, and enlightening guide.

* * *

At Imam Ghazali Publishing, our mission has always been to bring works of enduring spiritual and intellectual value to the English-speaking Muslim world. In an age where knowledge is often diluted or oversimplified, we have remained committed to publishing books that honor the depth and richness of our tradition while making them accessible to the modern reader.

The Qur'an Code is a natural extension of that mission. Just as we saw *The Endless Banquet* change lives by helping readers develop a relationship with the Qur'an, we believe *The Qur'an Code* will do the same—this time by deepening that relationship and unlocking new layers of meaning that have always been there, waiting to be discovered.

Our goal with this series is not just to publish thirty books, but to be part of a movement—a movement that revives the love of the Qur'an in the hearts of our readers. We want every reader to not only appreciate the beauty of the Qur'an but to feel empowered to engage with it on a profound level. This book is another step in that direction, another tool in the hands of those who long to understand and live by the divine words.

* * *

We invite you to embark on this journey with us. Whether you are reading this as someone who has already benefited from *The Endless Banquet* or as someone encountering our work for the first time, we promise you that *The Qur'an Code* will enrich your understanding of the Qur'an in ways you never imagined. It will make you see the Book of Allah with fresh eyes, uncover patterns you may have never noticed, and ultimately, draw you closer to its message.

The Qur'an is a limitless ocean of wisdom, and each of us is only at the shore. But with the right guidance, with the right tools, we can begin to wade deeper, to grasp more of its beauty, and to feel its transformative power in our lives.

This book is one of those tools. It is an invitation to decode the divine message, to see the order, the coherence, the brilliance of Allah's words in a way that strengthens both intellect and soul.

We are honored to present *The Qur'an Code* to you, and we pray that it serves as a means of increasing love, knowledge, and connection to the Qur'an for generations to come.

May Allah bless this effort of Shaykh Hamzah Abdul-Malik and grant us all deeper understanding of His Book. May we see him complete the entire series with ease and comfort.

May Allah bless the author and his family, the editors, the proofreaders, the typesetters, and all the members of our team at Imam Ghazali Publishing.

Anything indecorous in this rendering is from our own soul and our ignorance, and anything herein which is of benefit is from Allah. May Allah forgive us for our shortcomings, and may He bless all those who teach, read, and study all or part of this work, until the Day of Judgement. I end by asking that should you, the reader, benefit from this text, then kindly remember this poor and needy servant and his family in your supplications. *Āmīn*. All praise is due to Allah, Lord of the worlds.

Muhammad Adnaan Sattaur
Imam Ghazali Publishing

Sūrah al-Naba'

The Main Theme: Preparing for the Hereafter

Undoubtedly, the most pivotal event in life that most of humanity fails to prepare for is the Day of Resurrection. It is the decisive Day when our eternal fate of Heaven or Hell will be determined by our Creator. But it is also a day that many groups and peoples believe will *not* occur. This explains why the Day of Resurrection is one of the most recurring and powerful themes of the Qur'an.

Throughout the Quranic text, Allah f presents extensive evidence for why the Day of Resurrection will happen. Two key methods are employed by our Creator to achieve this end:

1) Demonstrating to us how He has made this entire universe function for us, and that we will in turn be held accountable and judged whether we showed appreciation for the gifts He has generously bestowed upon us.
2) Presenting clear and evident signs of resurrection in this world around us in a consistent fashion, which indicate how life appears after death.

Sūrah al-Naba' is a Quranic chapter that employs the first method to prove the resurrection in the next world. It even goes further by revealing some of the details of what will happen on the Day of Resurrection, as well as the comforts and torments that humanity will experience after they have been judged.

The Context: The Doubts of the Quraysh

The Quraysh used to constantly attempt to cast doubts and present refutations against the Prophet ﷺ, who warned his people of the Day of Resurrection. They would even go as far as challenging Allah Himself to impose the punishment early if it was certainly true! One example of this is al-Naḍr ibn al-Ḥārith, when he asked Allah mockingly, "If this claim of yours is really true, then rain down upon us stones from the sky or bring us a painful punishment!" (al-Wāḥidī) And sure enough, Allah answered his shameless call, as he was killed in the Battle of Badr. After the Muslims emerged victorious, the Prophet ﷺ asked the corpses of the former leaders of the disbelieving Quraysh, "We have found our Lord's promise to be true, so have you found your Lord's promise to be true as well?" (Muslim)

This is why this *sūrah* begins with a rhetorical question, "*What are they disputing with each other about?*" (*al-Naba'*, 1). This query demonstrates that the news of the Day of Resurrection is so great, so serious, and so well proven that it is baffling that anyone who sees its signs would doubt it at all, let alone challenge Allah f to make this Day come early or mock the Prophet ﷺ about it.

This was a major point of contention for the Quraysh, as they refused to believe in life after death at all. They used to taunt the Prophet by crumbling up decayed bones in their hands and mockingly asking, "... *who will give life to bones that have been decomposed?*" (*Yā Sīn*, 78) Hence, Allah dedicates this *sūrah* and many other chapters in this *juz'* to provide abundant proof that would leave no excuse for a person to disbelieve in it.

The Relationship with the Previous Sūrahs

The two *sūrahs* preceding Sūrah an-Naba' are al-Insān and al-Mursalāt. In those two *sūrahs*, Allah elucidates the experiences of Heaven and Hell, respectively, as if the reader is already living there with its inhabitants. The sights, sounds, food and drink, and emotions portrayed in those *sūrahs* paint a tangible picture of the pleasures and punishments that are promised in the Hereafter. As an extension of these golden themes, Sūrah an-Naba' directly connects its message to the promise made in the beginning of Sūrah al-Mursalāt.

1- The Irrationality of Disbelief

Allah says in Sūrah al-Mursalāt, "*Surely, what you are promised will come to pass*" (*al-Mursalāt*, 7), after swearing by undeniable signs such as the existence of clouds that hover above us everyday. The signs and manifestations of the Divine are so clear in Sūrah al-Mursalāt that Allah ends His call by saying, *"So what message, after this, would they believe in?"* (*al-Mursalāt*, 50). This indicates that the message could not be clearer for people who are reading this with an open mind. Consequently, Sūrah al-Naba' follows up the closing question expressed in Sūrah al-Mursalāt by questioning how the Quraysh can still disbelieve in the Last Day despite so many clear evidences being established. Yet, despite the fact that Allah already presented sufficient proof of the Day of Resurrection in Sūrah al-Mursalāt, He still reveals Sūrah al-Naba' with even more evidentiary indicators to appeal to people with common sense.

2- Our Humble Origins and Life

One of the main pieces of evidence found in Sūrahs al-Insān and al-Naba' that appeals to our common sense is our humble origin as human beings. Both *sūrahs* highlight our beginnings in similar ways, such as the verse, *"Indeed, We created humans from a drop of mixed fluids, Therefore, We gave him the faculties of hearing and sight"* (*al-Insān*, 2) in Sūrah al-Insān. In a parallel fashion, we find the verse *"Did We not create you from a humble fluid?"* (*al-Mursalāt*, 20) in Sūrah al-Mursalāt. Meanwhile, Sūrah al-Naba' takes us beyond our common reference points and draws our attention to all the evidences of the Divine around us.

3- Outcomes of the Day of Judgement

Another key defining theme of Sūrahs al-Insān and al-Mursalāt is that each *sūrah* expounds on only one of the two outcomes of the Day of Judgement. Sūrah al-Insān expounds on the life in Paradise while only briefly mentioning Hell, whereas Sūrahs al-Mursalāt expounds on the life of Hell while only briefly mentioning Paradise. Sūrah al-Naba' fuses these two poles together by balancing the description of Heaven and Hell in an even fashion. This neatly harmonizes our hopes and fears of Allah and the trials of the Last Day, such that we do not fall into complacency from Allah's magnanimous generosity nor fall into despair from His horrifying punishment.

Thematic Explanation of the Sūrah

Throughout the Qur'an, Allah establishes proof of His Lordship over us by establishing three categories of His infinite wisdom and planning:

1) Signs that He has brought us into existence, with this concept being expressed through the Arabic term *al-ījād* (الإيجاد).
2) Signs that He is the One Who prepared the Earth and universe for our benefit, which is encapsulated through the term *al-iᶜdād* (الإعداد).
3) Signs that he is the One Who created a perfect and balanced system that sustains us for generations, which is captured through the expression *al-imdād* (الإمداد).

In the first theme of this *sūrah*, Allah draw our attention to the evidence of *al-iᶜdād*. This is what we are supposed to consider when we read:

> "Is it not true that We have spread the earth like a bed, and the mountains as pegs, and created you in pairs, and made your sleep for rest, and made the night as a cloak, and made the day for livelihood, and we built above you seven firmaments, and have placed a lamp full of blazing splendour, and sent down from rainclouds pouring water, producing by it grain and various plants, and gardens of luxurious growth?" (*al-Naba'*, 6-16)

By attentively observing these signs, we should be able to clearly deduce that there is a system that has been put in place to prepare the Earth for our benefit. This mode of preparation was undertaken with absolute wisdom, knowledge, will, and power; these all constitute qualities of a Lord Who deserves to be worshiped and glorified. Once Allah has established that He is the One Who created the world for us, and that it was done with His full control, He then asserts that He can also change all these natural phenomena just as easily as He established them.

This draws us to the second theme, which in essence represents the next stage of life: the Day of Resurrection. In this context, we will notice that Allah shows us that He will radically change the world from its present and current setting. The same signs that He previously pointed us to will no longer serve our personal interests.

> "The Day of Decision is already fixed. On that Day, the Trumpet shall be sounded and you shall come forth in waves. The sky shall be opened as if there were doors. And the mountains shall vanish as if they were a mirage." (*al-Naba'*, 17-20)

The mountains that He made to previously stabilize our Earth will vanish and the sky He used to firmly protect us from the elements of space will open up entirely. Even more interestingly, we no longer will be paired by our biological attributes, but rather by the actions and beliefs we had in our previous life. This same theme is further emphasized at the end of the *sūrah*:

> "The Day that the Spirit and the angels will stand forth in ranks none shall speak except any who is permitted by (Allah) Most Gracious and he will say what is right. That Day is a sure reality. Let him who desires, seek a way back to his Lord. Indeed, We warn you of a doom at hand, a day whereon a man will look on that which his own hands have sent before, and the disbeliever will cry: 'Would that I were dust!'" (*al-Naba'*, 38-40)

With regard to the third theme, Allah presents to us the two final destinations where people will eternally reside.

First and foremost, Allah introduces the destination that disbelievers will encounter: Jahannam. Just as Allah had previously prepared the Earth in our first life to comprehensively work in our favour, He also meticulously designed Jahannam to function in every possible way to torment its inhabitants in the Hereafter.

> "For sure, Hell shall lie in ambush, to become a home for the transgressors. There they shall live for endless ages. There they will not taste any coolness or drink, except scalding water and decaying filth. This is a reward proportioned (to their evil deeds)." (*al-Naba'*, 20-26)

Closing the subject of Jahannam, Allah highlights in express terms how this reward was proportionate to the deeds that they committed in the first life:

> "They never expected to be held accountable. And they totally rejected our signs. But We had recorded everything precisely in a Book. So it will be said to them, 'Taste the fruits of your deeds! You shall have nothing but increase in punishment.'" (*al-Naba'*, 27-30)

On the other hand, Allah makes it abundantly clear to His servants that Jannah was meticulously designed to provide every pleasure imaginable, and that this privilege is reserved for people who led righteous lives in the temporal world:

> "On that Day, the righteous will certainly achieve their heart's desires: luxuriant gardens and vineyards, and splendid companions well-matched, and overflowing cups. They shall hear no vanity, nor any falsehood; a reward as a generous gift from your Lord." (*al-Naba'*, 30-36)

One fine point we observe in this segment is that Allah described the punishment of Jahannam as "proportionate" while labelling the pleasures of Jannah as "a generous gift". This demonstrates to us that even in the Hereafter, Allah is still merciful with us by not punishing people beyond what is justly due to them while rewarding people beyond what they deserve.

In conclusion, Sūrah al-Naba' provides us a well-rounded understanding of why the Day of Resurrection is so vital and must be believed in with full certainty. This *sūrah* shows us that all the blessings of this first life come with a responsibility that we will be held accountable for in the Hereafter. It also demonstrates that Allah's relationship with us is based on mercy and forgiveness, without sacrificing justice for those who do not care about taking their lives or the lives of others seriously. And finally, it demonstrates the importance of taking this message to heart now in this life while we can will certainly influence our moral standing in the next life. As for those who refuse to take heed of all the signs around them and the warnings of the permanent consequences to come, it is sufficient for us to know that the truth will always prevail. As Allah says unequivocally, *"Verily they shall soon (come to) know! And again, they shall soon come to know!"* (*al-Naba'*, 4-5)

Sūrah al-Nāziʿāt

The Main Theme: Dispelling Self-Delusion

When human beings become heedless and fail to recognize their true Creator, they inevitably begin to lie to themselves about the nature of their present state as well as the fate they will inevitably face in the future. Hence, this *sūrah* is dedicated to dispelling and correcting all of these self-made delusions, especially misunderstandings about human nature and life after death.

Humans who encounter the message of guidance will ultimately fall under one of two categories: 1) those who believe in the message, and 2) those who disbelieve. Sūrah al-Nāziʿāt is dedicated to addressing those who disbelieve in the true message by challenging their delusions with respect to 1) the nature of this world, 2) the nature of humanity, and 3) the nature of life after death. These three misconceptions of the disbelievers are addressed in the aforementioned order.

This order is appropriate, since as an empirical reality, most misguidance starts by allowing ignorance to dictate how we view the world and its purpose. In accordance with that view, we define ourselves when delineating our relationship and understanding of the world around us. Our understanding of the world and our own selves will then shape our understanding of the nature and purpose of death, as well as the question of whether there is life after death. Without divine guidance from the unseen realm, most people are likely to have misgivings and construct gross fantasies of who their Lord is, to the extent that some might even claim to be lords themselves. Accordingly, Allah revealed Sūrah al-Nāziʿāt to correct such grave misunderstandings and unequivocally describe the destiny of those who decide to ignore the truth when it is presented to them.

The Context: When will the Day Come?

The Prophet ﷺ was unrelenting and committed to sharing the message of the Qur'an with his people. And, as we established in the previous chapter, one of the most common themes of the Qur'an is the Day of Resurrection. The insistence of the Prophet ﷺ towards reminding his people of this Day annoyed the Quraysh and they, like the disbelievers before them, clamoured to refute his claim. Although the Qur'an presents a plethora of proofs ranging from as far as the stars in the universe to something as close to us as our own embryological origins, they were all generally ignored by the opponents of the Prophet ﷺ. Instead, they fell into the same illogical pitfall as many people before them did when they were warned of an impending punishment by asking, "*...when will this threat come to pass, if what you say is true?*" (*Yā Sīn*, 48)

Therefore, Allah devotes much of this *sūrah* to addressing this problematic sentiment articulated by the disbelievers. In fact, Allah brings this subject up explicitly in the *sūrah* by stating, "*They ask you regarding the Hour, 'When will it be?'*" (*al-Nāziʿāt*, 42). The truth that we ultimately derive from this discussion is that *knowing* when the Day will occur is not nearly as important as being *prepared* for it. In fact, knowing when it will occur will likely only increase complacency of the people; in such a case, a person will assume that they have time, or even worse, disbelieve in it and arrogantly wait until the appointed time actually comes, just for the chance of disproving it if it does not occur.

Moreover, knowing the terrifying events that the Day of Judgement entails and the dire stakes of eternal punishment or pleasure should actually suffice us from our concerns of knowing when it it will occur. This is because no amount of time will ever really be sufficient enough for us to fully prepare for it without Allah's mercy. Thus, only those of us who take heed to its seriousness will benefit from the warning, for, as Allah says, "*Your duty is only to warn whoever is in awe of it.*" (*al-Nāziʿāt*, 79:45)

May Allah make us among those who are in awe of that Day in this worldly life so that we will be engulfed in His Mercy during that pressing time.

The Relationship with Sūrah al-Naba'

Sūrah al-Nāziʿāt – like many of the *sūrahs* in this *juz'* – follows the same theme as Sūrah al-Naba', namely warning us about the Day of Judgement. However, this does not mean that Sūrah al-Nāziʿāt is redundant. Rather, Sūrah al-Nāziʿāt provides details on key issues that Sūrah al-Naba' only addresses in general.

After undertaking a close comparative study, we find that Sūrah al-Nāziʿāt complements Sūrah al-Naba' perfectly. In the latter, Allah only makes the claim that the Day of Judgement will happen as a promise, but then in Sūrah al-Nāziʿāt Allah renders this promise complete by swearing upon it. This adds even more gravity to the word of surety made in Sūrah al-Naba'.

Furthermore, in Sūrah al-Naba' Allah draws to our attention the environmental changes that will be introduced on the Day of Resurrection and only brings up the state of the disbeliever at the very end, saying, "... *and the disbeliever will cry: 'Would that I were dust!'*" (*al-Naba'*, 40). Meanwhile, in Sūrah al-Nāziʿāt Allah lays out the intricacies of the psychological state of the disbelievers relatively early in the chapter, as if this theme is flowing directly from the ending point of Sūrah al-Naba'.

Another key observation that could be made is the intricate connection found between the beginning literary themes of both *sūrahs*. In Sūrah al-Naba', Allah promises twice that the disbelievers will regret their denial of the Day of Resurrection, "*Verily they shall soon (come to) know! And again, they shall soon come to know!*" (al-Naba', 4-5) And as we already know, Sūrah al-Naba' demonstrates why they will regret it by describing the Day of Resurrection, Heaven, and Hell. On the other hand, in Sūrah al-Nāziʿāt Allah highlights a different temporal point wherein they will regret their denial of the Resurrection: the very moment when death will come to them and take their souls. However, this connection would apply only if we interpreted the beginning of Sūrah al-Nāziʿāt as a rhetorical description of the angels of death.

Another way that the two *sūrahs* complement each other is that in Sūrah al-Naba' Allah depicts a lucid picture of the state of people in Hell and Paradise, whereby most of the chapter is devoted to providing their respective descriptions. Yet, it is equally important for us to see concrete examples of the worldly paths that lead the people to those destinations. For this reason, Allah dedicates a significant portion of Sūrah al-Nāziʿāt towards providing us specific examples of distinguished individuals – whether in a positive or negative sense – who are well-known throughout history who embody the highest traits of people who ultimately become the residents of Heaven and Hell.

Thematic Explanation of the Sūrah

The first theme that stands out in this *sūrah* is that Allah swears by a number of distinguished members of His creation in the first several *āyāt*. A noteworthy fact in this regard is that this is the very first *sūrah* in this *juz'* that begins with swearing, but what is even more significant is the nature of the beings that Allah is swearing by.

Oftentimes in the Qur'an, Allah will commence a *sūrah* by swearing on specific places, people, or things. However, in this *sūrah* Allah swears in relatively ambiguous terms; He purposely does this in order to incorporate many different meanings and spiritual lessons at the same time, such that the lesson is relevant to every reader's experience. Another wisdom that is ingrained within this approach is that it allows us to incorporate the ambiguous terms to any new appropriate components or contexts that may appear over time. This enables us to strengthen our faith in every era and allows the message to be relevant for every generation of believers. Therefore, it is no surprise to find that the scholars differ on what the initial verses of the chapter refer to. Some scholars state that He is swearing by the Angels, whereby the following interpretation would be yielded:

> "I swear by those Angels who violently pull out the souls, and by those who pull out the souls gently, and by the order-bearing Angels gliding swiftly down, then race headlong to carry out the commands of Allah, and by those Angels conducting the commands." (*al-Nāziʿāt*, 1-5)

Other scholars interpreted the initial sequence to refer to planets and stars, such that the interpretation would look like this:

> "I swear by those [stars] that rise only to set, and move [in their orbits] with steady motion, and float [through space] with floating serene, and yet pass [one another] swiftly: and thus they fulfill the [Creator's] command!" (*al-Nāziʿāt*, 1-5)

Most interestingly, there are other interpretations as well. Nevertheless, the unifying principle behind all these exegetical views is the same: Allah is swearing by the inescapable laws or protocols that govern our lives, whether that is from the unseen realm (i.e. the Angels in charge of death and sustenance) or the observable and empirical realm (i.e. the Sun, Moon, and the constellations we use for navigation, pinpointing the time, and determining the seasons). Since we genuinely consider the undeniable laws that govern the observable realm and live according to how it will affect our worldly trajectory, it behooves us to know the laws that govern the unseen realm, just like the moment of our death and the Day of Resurrection. That way, we can lead our lives according to how they will affect our eternal destiny.

This is why Allah brings us directly to the second theme, namely the state of those who failed to live according to the laws of the unseen realm. The individuals who denied the message and disregarded life after death will be overwhelmed with shock and regret once they realize that they erred about the truth and magnitude of this Day.

> "The Day on which the quake shall cause a violent convulsion, which will be followed by another violent convulsion, and on that Day, hearts shall be pounding with terror, with their eyes downcast, saying, 'What! We have been returned to our former state? Even though we had become a heap of hollow crumbling bones?' They will further say: 'Then such a return would be a total loss for us!' But indeed, it will take only one mighty Blast, and at once they will be above ground.'" (*al-Nāziʿāt*, 6-14)

Allah then brings our attention to the the most poignant example of a person in denial of this outcome. He is none other than Firʿawn, the tyrannical Pharaoh who ruled over Egypt. Firʿawn is the perfect example of a person who had every material advantage that a person could desire in this world while also being a person who did everything he could to reject the message of the Allah. He stubbornly remained on the path of falsehood despite the most extensive measures being taken to convince him of the true message of monotheism and the Lordship of Allah.

> "Has word reached you of Moses? When his Lord called him in the sacred valley of Ṭuwā: 'Go unto Pharaoh – for, verily, he has utterly transgressed. And tell him, "Have you the desire to purify yourself? And for me to guide you to your Lord so that you will be in awe of Him?"' So Moses showed him the supreme wondrous sign. But Pharaoh cried lies and disobeyed; and worse, turned his back, striving his worst against him. Then he assembled his magicians and proclaimed to all saying, 'I am your highest lord of all your gods.' So Allah took him to task, and made him a terrifying example in the life to come as well as in this world. Surely in this is a lesson for whoever stands in awe of Allah." (*al-Nāziʿāt*, 15-26)

One of the key reasons why disbelievers find the concept of resurrection to be so far-fetched lies in the assumption that the human being's physical and mental constitution is so complicated and advanced that it would be near impossible to recreate us at all, let alone recreate us in the exact form we assumed in the temporal world. Ironically, despite articulating this blatant disbelief in Allah's abilities, many people are still vain enough to believe in their own abilities to perform this undertaking themselves. And some take this delusion even further by embracing the philosophy of transhumanism, which entails believing that we can make even better versions of humans than those that Allah has created. These delusions of omnipotence and self-importance reflect the same type of disbelief embraced by Firʿawn, which ultimately led to his disbelief in Allah and the Last Day. As a result, Allah dispels these vain notions of human grandeur and material success by articulating an *a fortiori* argument that would appeal to all of us:

> "Were all of you then harder to create, or the very sky above? He built it! Raised its height to the utmost aloft, and perfected it to

a finish; darkened its night deepest black, and brought forth its resplendent midmorning sun. And the earth after all that, He smoothed it out fair to dwell upon. He brought forth its water and rich pasturage. And the mountains He anchored firm. All of this was done as a tremendous but passing means of livelihood for you and your animals." (*al-Nāziʿāt*, 27-33)

In these *āyāt*, Allah not only logically demonstrates that He is more than capable of creating us, but He also evidences His control over the entire universe and cosmos. This is why He draws our attention back to the fundamental logical basis of the Day of Resurrection; for if He is the One Who created and controls the laws of nature in this life, then how can one conceivably doubt in His promise of transforming the world and resurrecting us on the Day of Judgement? Imagine how utterly dismayed people will be on that Day after realizing that they should have followed the intuitive and cogent arguments Allah is presenting to them and believed that this Day would come. The golden rule is this: if a person waits until the Day of Judgement to believe, it will be far too late, for only those who prepared for that fateful moment beforehand will prosper.

"So when the absolute devastation comes; the Day when Man will call to mind all that he had striven for, and when the raging blaze of hell shall be laid bare for any to see; then, he who had rebelled, and preferred the pathetic life of this world, verily that raging blaze will be his home! But as for him who feared to stand before his Lord and restrained his soul from its whims, the lush grove of paradise will certainly be his home." (*al-Nāziʿāt*, 34-39)

In conclusion, Allah closes this decisive chapter by reminding us of our human limitations, and teaches us that even the Prophet ﷺ himself has limitations in what he can do. For instance, he did not possess the faculty to make all people believe in the message of Islam, regardless of his eagerness and efforts. Allah reminds him of this reality, which is why it makes no difference if he knows when the Day of Judgement will happen. This is because as a logical truth, we will all die before it happens. Thus, no matter how sooner or later it is, the people who deny it will find that it will come much sooner than they expect.

"They mockingly ask you about the Last Hour: 'When will it come?' In what position are you to speak of it? To your Lord alone does its knowledge end. Your duty is only to be a warner to those whom it fills with awe. On the Day they see it, it will be as if they had stayed in the world no more than the wane of a day, or the blaze of the morning sun." (*al-Nāziʿāt*, 42-46)

Sūrah ʿAbasa

Main Theme

One of the most difficult questions that emerge when inviting people to guidance (*daʿwah*) is determining how effective we are in relaying the divine message of Islam. Sometimes we might think that we are being too aggressive in our approach, while in other circumstances we might feel that we are being too careful. There will be times where we might assume we gave *daʿwah* at the wrong time, and in other situations we might feel we missed the best opportunity to speak in a frank and transparent fashion. In such cases, we question whether we have spent too much time patiently addressing every argument a skeptic has proffered, and at the same time we might blame ourselves for not spending enough time to convince a person of the true message of Islam. Ultimately, one of the worst fears we could have is presuming that we misrepresented the message to the extent that we pushed a person even further from Islam than their original baseline position.

All these concerns are natural and understandable, because representing the message is a formidable responsibility. After all, we are representing the message of the Creator f and His Prophet ﷺ. In such a context, making an egotistical mistake could cost us our own salvation in the Hereafter. Moreover, in such interactions the stakes are extremely high, for we naturally feel that if we successfully guide someone, then that person will go to Paradise and we will possibly gain the reward. Conversely, we suppose that if we fail in that regard, then that person could possibly go to Hell for eternity, and we might be questioned about how we preached the message to them.

No human being was more concerned about the delivery of his message than the Prophet Muhammad ﷺ. Since he ﷺ had seen the horrors of Hell before his very own eyes, he, more than anyone, had iron-clad certainty with regard to the consequences of rejecting this message. Moreover, his love for humanity was unparalleled and unequalled to the extent that he would become depressed when he could not convince a person to save themselves from the fire of Hell. For as Allah states: *"Now, perhaps you might well slay yourself out of sheer regret, left standing in their tracks behind them, if they continue to disbelieve in this message."* (*al-Kahf*, 6)

Accordingly, Allah revealed Sūrah ʿAbasa to comfort every person who has these concerns. Within its powerful verses, He teaches us that the Qur'an is self-sufficient in its reminders and exhortations, and that a person can - and will - be guided if they are sincerely looking for guidance. *"But no! This revelation is an incomparably powerful reminder. So, whoever is willing may remember it."* (*ʿAbasa*, 11-12)

In other words, the quality of our proselytization techniques will not affect the general outcome of their belief or disbelief, for such a result is outside of our control. Rather, we are only morally responsible for sharing the message to every accessible member of humanity with sincerity and relative wisdom, regardless of the outcome. Beyond that, we should prioritize our time and resources to teaching those who are wholeheartedly sincere and eager to learn, and leave the consequences to our Maker. The only heart we can control is our own, so our primary responsibility should be to keep our own spiritual disposition in the right place, thereby hoping that Allah will give us all the best outcome on the Day of Reckoning. For as one key Quranic verse states: *"And do not disgrace me on the Day all will be resurrected - the Day when neither wealth nor children will be of any benefit. Only those who come before Allah with a pure heart will be saved."* (*al-Shuʿarā'*, 87-89)

The Context: Who Benefits from Guidance?

The Prophet ﷺ was assigned the heavy and unprecedented responsibility of being a Messenger to all people, which *ipso facto* included the rich and poor, old and young, as well as the Arab and non-Arab categories. However, with this responsibility he sometimes faced a critical dilemma: which group among the aforementioned categories requires and deserves most of his attention and time for learning the message?

At a *prima facie* level, a clear-cut answer was not available for this pressing problem. On the one hand, the downtrodden, such as the poor and the slaves, were urgently in need of liberation and support at both the spiritual and social levels. The Qur'an advocated for social justice, fairness, and ethnic equality under the divine laws of Allah. They were also most receptive to the message of Islam because it provided an egalitarian worldview that instilled dignity in their hearts, increased their spiritual confidence in this world, and provided them hope for a better life for all the worldly struggles they faced. In fact, this was the most common societal group that followed the previous Prophets عليهم السلام in history, and they usually became the moral leaders of religious society, for Allah states: *"And We desired to show favor unto those who were oppressed in the earth, and to make them examples and to make them the inheritors."* (*al-Qaṣaṣ*, 5)

On the other hand, the Prophet ﷺ also had intimate ties and interactions with the leaders of the Quraysh, as he appreciated the political influence that each of them exerted over their respective tribes. He believed that the conversion of a single leader could drastically change the political landscape in favour of the nascent Muslim community in general, and tremendously alleviate the suffering of the poor and reduce the torture of Muslims at a more specific level. Furthermore, the conversion of tribal leaders like al-Ṭufayl ibn ʿAmr h became the direct cause and decisive factor in having their entire clans embrace Islam, and no one but Allah knew how close any them were to accepting Islam.

This was the very context in which Sūrah ʿAbasa was revealed.

It was during the early period of Islam – namely the Meccan setting – when these considerations were most crucial. The Muslims were few in number and many of them faced the immediate threat of death and torture. In most cases, the disbelieving clan leaders were not willing to engage with the Prophet ﷺ in any capacity or listen to his message at all. Hence, when the Prophet ﷺ was presented with the rare opportunity to teach Islam to an entire group of the most influential leaders of Mecca, which included Abū Jahl and his own uncle al-ʿAbbās h, he sought to engage with them immediately. The Prophet ﷺ took full advantage of the unprecedented moment and provided them his undivided attention, for if his message could penetrate the heart of even one of them, the entire Muslim community would gain mass support and rejoice in victory.

As he was nearing the crucial turning point of the conversation, it appeared that he was on the verge of reaching a breakthrough with one of them. And it was at this very sensitive moment that one of his followers, ʿAbdullāh ibn Umm Maktūm h, a blind man, interrupted him and approached him with a question. The story is narrated in full in the following Hadith:

"ʿAbdullāh ibn Umm Maktūm came to the Prophet ﷺ and began to say, 'O Muhammad, show me a place near you (so you can teach me),' whilst one of the leading men of the idol worshippers was in audience with the Prophet ﷺ. The Prophet ﷺ began to turn away from him and give his attention to the other man, and he said to him, 'Father of so-and-so, do you see any harm in what I am saying?' and he said, 'No, by the blood (of our sacrifices) I see no harm in what you are saying.' And then Sūrah ʿAbasa – 'He frowned and turned away when the blind man came' – was sent down." (Muwaṭṭa' Mālik)

Allah revealed this *sūrah* to teach the Prophet ﷺ that no matter how socially important a person is, as long as they insist on clinging to disbelief they should never be assigned precedence over a person whose heart is already open to guidance. This was a critical lesson for the Muslim nation and the Prophet ﷺ reminded us of this lesson, for whenever he saw ʿAbdullāh ibn Umm Maktūm h, he would affectionately say, "Welcome to the one on whose account my Lord rebuked me!" The Prophet ﷺ further honoured him by giving him a rank beside Bilāl h as the caller to prayer (*mu'adhdhhin*). Among the highest honours that the Prophet ﷺ gave him was that he would leave him in charge of the entire city of Madina in his absence. As for the leaders who rejected the prophetic message back in Mecca, they ultimately persisted in their disbelief of the message of Islam until their death. Their legacies fell from grace in this life and they will find an even worse destination and fate in the next abode.

This is a lesson for all individuals engaged in the field of *daʿwah*. We never know what Allah has in store for a person, but this *sūrah* teaches us that regardless of how important some people might seem to be at the social level, their true value lies in their commitment to truth and guidance, and these characteristics will always be prioritized and favoured by Allah in this life and in the next.

Relationship with Sūrah al-Nāziʿāt

In Sūrah al-Nāziʿāt, Allah provides us a clear example of the qualities of the disbelievers in the story of Pharaoh. Through the tale of the latter, He demonstrates how a person's free will to be arrogant can cause them to ignore the most undeniable of miracles and signs, like those presented by Prophet Mūsā ﷺ. This story demonstrates that if a person chooses not to fear the station of his Lord, then nothing can make him believe. Hence, Sūrah al-Nāziʿāt ends with the following address, *"Your duty is only to be a warner to those whom it [the Day of Resurrection] fills with awe."* [*al-Nāziʿāt*, 45] In other words, this message will only prove to be effective for individuals who believe in the possibility of life after death and genuinely feel a sense of fear of accountability vis-à-vis the afterlife. Hence, Allah introduces to us Sūrah ʿAbasa to give us an example of a person who fits this description of belief via the story of ʿAbdullāh ibn Umm Maktūm h.

Another striking connection worthy of mention is that Sūrah al-Nāziʿāt briefly highlights the creation of the Earth as a sign of His favour and power over us when He said, *"He brought forth its water and rich pasturage."* (*al-Nāziʿāt*, 30) Allah further expounds upon this point in rich detail, as we will see in the Thematic Explanation of the *sūrah*.

Lastly, while in Sūrah al-Nāziʿāt Allah draws our attention to the psychological state of the disbelievers, in Sūrah ʿAbasa He goes beyond their personal feelings about themselves and depicts to us how this Day affects the relationships between them and those who they held dear in this world.

Ultimately, upon reading the two *sūrahs*, we will come to the realization that Sūrah ʿAbasa broadens our understanding of the Day of Resurrection. For it provides us an even more comprehensive picture of both the blessings Allah has bestowed upon us in the world, as well as making the Day of Judgement more vivid than we previously imagined.

The Thematic Explanation of the Sūrah

Sūrah ʿAbasa begins by grounding us in the understanding of how guidance works by juxtaposing it with futile methods. Essentially, the effectiveness of any religious call is contingent on the mindset of the person who is receiving it. If the person is receptive and seeks spiritual purification, then the message of guidance will yield fruits. But if a person is bent on arrogance and ignorance, no amount of evidence will move them.

If we accept this state of affairs, it becomes abundantly clear that we should prioritize our attention in favour of those who seek guidance over those who reject it in contexts when we must make a choice between the two. This is the fact of the matter, regardless of what the political and social situation might seem to suggest. Internalizing this reality is the responsibility of anyone who teaches the divine message: it is their obligation to deliver it with full integrity and honesty, and it is the obligation of the recipient to receive it in good faith. Subsequently, both sides will be taken to account accordingly. This is the very moral lesson that Allah teaches us in the first part of the *sūrah*:

> "He frowned and turned away, because the blind man approached him. How could you tell? He might have sought to purify himself, or he may be mindful, benefitting from the reminder. As to one who regards himself as self-sufficient, you gave him your attention, even though you are not to blame if he would not purify himself. But as to him who came to thee striving earnestly, being in awe, from him you were distracted. But no! This [revelation] is truly a reminder. And so, whoever is willing may remember it." (*ʿAbasa*, 1-12)

The next segment demonstrates why the Qur'an cannot be embraced by a heart that has been submerged in darkness and is committed to denying the truth. Allah teaches us that, by its very nature, the Qur'an is purifying light: "*...There certainly has come to you from Allah a light and a clear Book.*" (*al-Mā'idah*, 15) Such a bright and pristine light is only compatible with pure things. This is the case regardless of whether it is the physical purity of the pages it is written on, the hands that hold them, or the hearts of people seeking to purify themselves by submitting to the truth. In an enlightening passage of this chapter, He describes the purity of everything that beholds it:

> "It is in celestial-inscribed pages high in honor. Lofty of rank, pristine in inviolate sacred purity. In the hands of legion angelic

> bearers of revelation; supremely noble, devoted to Him with every good." (*'Abasa*, 13-16)

This explains why it is such a dire sign for people who are averse to this Reminder. It can only be an indicator of a woeful darkness in their hearts that will inevitably lead to damnation and self-destruction in the afterlife. The only reason for why people would deny the speech of the Divine is if they incorrectly deduce that they have some power to control their destiny. Thus, Allah reminds us to use our intellect and consider our humble origin so that we might rely on our basic intuitions and realize that our resurrection will occur just as easily as we were created the first time. We would only be doing ourselves a grave disservice if we oppose the One Who brought us into existence.

> "Man is (self) destroyed: how ungrateful! From what did He create him? From a mere sperm drop He created him and perfected him to measure. Then and greater, He makes it easy for him to go through life. Then and yet greater, He causes them to die and be buried. And finally and even greater, when He wills, He shall raise him again to life." (*'Abasa*, 17-22)

It is sufficiently condemnable that people would deny their fate of resurrection in the permanent plane of the afterlife. But what is even more daunting is the fact that these same people will soon learn that the provisions of this current world were not provided to them for mere self-amusement. Rather, every meticulously arranged provision that Allah has allotted in this temporal world comes with the responsibility of us having the decency to show gratitude. Put in another way, our ingratitude in this life will put us in an even more wretched position once we are resurrected and questioned about what we did with this generous life bestowed to us by Allah.

> "By no means has he fulfilled the duty that Allah had assigned him. Let man, then, consider his food: How We pour down rainwater in abundance, and meticulously split the earth open, causing grain to grow in it, and grapes and green fodder, and olive trees and

> date-palms, and dense orchards, and fruits and herbage, for you and for your animals to enjoy." (*ʿAbasa*, 23-32)

After spending an entire lifetime submerged in a state of ungratefulness notwithstanding all these immaculate blessings, what amount of darkness would accumulate in a person's heart who rejected Allah's guidance? This is the very danger that individuals like ʿAbdullāh ibn Umm Maktūm h were seeking refuge from. Both he and many others like him rushed towards the light of truth in this world so they could purify their hearts and prepare themselves for the Reckoning. As for those who reject the truth, Allah provides the crystal-clear declaration that it is ultimately their loss, and on the Day of Resurrection their inner darkness will cause them to continue running away from the truth. Their ordeal on the Day of Judgement will be so severe that they will flee even from the very people who used to give them a sense of security in this world.

Such is the destiny of those who sincerely pursued the truth as opposed to those who arrogantly rejected it. This latter topic is echoed in the end of Sūrah ʿAbasa:

> "Finally when there comes the deafening blast, on that Day each man shall flee from his own brother, and from his mother and father, and from his spouse and his children: for every last one of them will have too weighty a care for anything else. A great many faces on that Day shall be beaming. Smiling with joyous laughter, glowing with expectation. And a great many faces on that day shall be grimed with dust, and veiled with dark despair. Those are the godless deniers." (*ʿAbasa*, 33-42)

RESERVE
FEDERAL
RESERVE
20
MG53264757C
SERIES 2013
OF AMERICA

Sūrah al-Takwīr

The Main Theme

Undoubtedly, one of the greatest blessings of the Qur'an is that Allah bestows us an overabundance of knowledge regarding the unseen realm, and this is especially true when it comes to describing the Day of Resurrection. The depictions are so graphic, vivid, and impactful that if people studied the Qur'an closely, they would have as much – or even more – certainty in the truth of the Day of Resurrection as they would have in everything that is currently occurring around them in the physical world.

Sūrah al-Takwīr is one of three *sūrahs* that will undoubtedly give us this kind of certainty in the Resurrection if we sincerely seek it and search for it. The Prophet ﷺ said, "Whoever wishes to look at the Day of Resurrection, as if he is seeing it with this own eyes, then let him recite 'When the Sun is folded' (*al-Takwīr*), 'When the heaven is cleft asunder' (*al-Infiṭār*), and 'When the heaven is split asunder' (*al-Inshiqāq*)." (al-Tirmidhī)

In its scope and subject matter, Sūrah al-Takwīr is unique insofar as it takes us far beyond addressing the earlier questions of *when* the Day of Judgement will happen, and instead orients us to *what* happens, which is far more important. Upon reading this *sūrah*, one gains the impression that a person's disbelief in the Day of Resurrection is inconsequential to its inevitability. This is commensurate to how a person's disbelief of the Sun rising will not change the undeniable fact that it will still happen.

This is why Allah emphasizes the concept of trust in this *sūrah*. We must maintain full confidence in the promises articulated in the Qur'an, the character of the Prophet ﷺ, and the angelic forces of the unseen realm. By developing that trust, we will naturally internalize the fact that the Day of Resurrection is real. Trust is the foundation upon which certainty is built, and that foundation should be rooted in the most honourable and trustworthy of sources. Put simply, the more truthful our source of trust is, the stronger our level of certainty can be. It is Sūrah al-Takwīr that gives us the information we need to keep that epistemic certitude firmly rooted.

The Context: Who is in Control?

One of the most common flaws of misguidance is the notion that we must rely solely on ourselves to become righteous and lead moral lives. Although it is true that we must make a commitment and sincere effort to become better, ultimately, our will is still dependent on our relationship with Allah. After all, without His will, we cannot fulfil our aspirations of being on the straight path.

This is one of the fatal misconceptions that the leaders of the Quraysh articulated in their discourses. They did not believe that they needed Allah to become righteous, and instead asserted that the pagan tradition of their forefathers sufficed them. The Prophet ﷺ was sent to dispel such notions. Hence, when the *āyah* of Sūrah al-Takwīr was revealed, "*Verily this is no less than a Message to (all) the Worlds: to whoever of you wills to take the Straight Way*" (*al-Takwīr*, 27-28), Abū Jahl voiced this sentiment of spiritual self-sufficiency by replying, "The matter is entirely up to us: if we so willed, we can rectify ourselves, and if we so willed we could decide to not rectify ourselves." In response, Allah corrected him and revealed the next *āyah*, "*But you cannot will it unless Allah, the Sustainer of all the worlds, wills to show you that way.*" (*al-Takwīr*, 29)

The Relationship with Sūrah ʿAbasa

Sūrah ʿAbasa, as well as Sūrah al-Nāziʿāt before it, both conclude with a chilling warning of the impending doom of the Day of Resurrection, but each emphasizes different aspects of the Final Day. Sūrah al-Nāziʿāt describes it as "The Overwhelming Event" (*al-Ṭāmmah*) while Sūrah ʿAbasa describes it as "The Deafening Blast" (*al-Ṣākhkhah*). Each *sūrah* gives us various descriptions of the horrifying events that will occur on the Day of Judgement. This is not to confuse us, but rather to underscore the fact that this Day will be unlike anything that we have ever experienced or imagined. Everything about this Day will be tremendously shocking, which is why its horrors cannot be emphasized enough. Hence, to give us a full and comprehensive picture Allah dedicates several *sūrahs* to elaborately pinpoint the many different ways the world will change on the Day of Judgement. This is why Allah says in Sūrah ʿAbasa, "*On that Day each man shall flee from his own brother, and from his mother and father, and from his spouse and his children. For each one of them, on that Day, shall have enough concern of his own to make him indifferent to the others.*" (ʿ*Abasa*, 37)

What kind of situation would be so terrifying that a person would be willing to run away from their own parents, children, and spouse? What would need to happen for people to be so selfish that they would not even care about the fate of their own family? Allah does not leave these questions unanswered, which is why He dedicates al-Takwīr to giving us more details of the supernatural shifts that will radically transform our relationships.

Thematic Explanation of the Sūrah

Sūrah al-Takwīr commences by giving us another elaborate portrait of the Day of Judgement. This time, we notice the consistent pattern of the upending of natural laws, whereby everything will appear to function in the opposite way it does in this temporal world. As human beings, we thrive and draw comfort in stable environments where things are mostly predictable, operate in a regulated and fixed manner, and work in our best interest. In Sūrah al-Takwīr, however, everything above us, below us, and around us will be in disarray, and we will almost immediately become aware of the stark contrast from the world we once knew. At that pivotal moment, every member of creation will know that it was always He Who controlled and regulated the cosmos.

> "When the Sun (with its spacious light) is folded up, and when the ascendent stars plunge down spent and dark, and when the mountains are blown adrift, and when full-pregnant camels are utterly abandoned, when the wild beasts are massed for their retribution, when the seas are stoked roaring with a fire, when the souls are joined with like, and when the infant girl that was buried alive is asked, for what sin was she slain?" (*al-Takwīr*, 1-9)

As we observe in the last *āyah* of that section, soon after witnessing the destruction of the Earth as we know it, we will realize that everyone will be either fleeing from their counterparts or looking for justice. The seekers of justice and demanders of retribution will even include children who were killed before they could speak. As overwhelming as this spectacle is, Allah draws our attention to the fact that all these mind-blowing and awesome cosmic changes are just a prelude for something even more tremendous, namely the Reckoning that He had warned us was an inescapable reality. In fact, on that decisive Day, everyone will intuitively know what is about to happen without being told; with the mere sight of the preparations being made, they will begin to calculate their chances of attaining salvation and will anxiously await the judgement of their Creator:

> "...and when the records of deeds are laid open to see, and when the sky is peeled back, and when the raging Hell is fiercely flared up, and when the lush grove of Paradise will be brought near: on that Day every human being will come to know what he has prepared for himself." (*al-Takwīr*, 10-14)

In this context, we should note that for the disbelievers hearing this dramatic and moving description, the events are so counterintuitive to their ignorant and slanted presuppositions that they will try to find any excuse to disbelieve in it, and even call the sanity of the Messenger ﷺ into question. They will likely pose a number of rhetorical questions to justify their doubts, such as the following: "How is this even possible? Where is he getting this information from? How could the world change so drastically?"

Allah upends all these aforementioned doubts by citing the empirical evidences of the world around them. He Himself also bears witness to the fact that He alone is the source of the knowledge of the Prophet ﷺ. The Quraysh cannot cogently contest this point, since they already know fully well that he was not a liar, a quality which they never once accused him of possessing.

> "But no! I need not even swear by the retreating stars, that run their course and set, and by the night as it darkly falls, and by the dawn as it breathes away the darkness; verily this word is brought by a

> noble angelic Messenger, possessor of mighty power, high-placed with Him on the Throne, obeyed there in heaven, faithfully true in delivering his trust. Nor is your companion any madman. Verily, he did see him (Jibrīl) in the limitless clear sky. Nor ever would he stingily withhold what is revealed to him of the unseen. Nor is it the word of an outcast devil. So where do you get by rejecting its truth?" (*al-Takwīr*,15-26)

In conclusion, Allah brings us back to the same central point that He has reiterated several times in His Word: that this reminder is meant for anyone who wants to prepare themselves for what is to come. This is just as He said in Sūrah ʿAbasa, *"But no! This [revelation] is truly a reminder. And so, whoever is willing may remember it"* (*ʿAbasa*, 11-12) as well as in Sūrah *al-Nāziʿāt*, *"Your duty is only to be a warner to those whom it fills with awe."* (*al-Nāziʿāt*, 45) But this time in Sūrah al-Takwīr, Allah adds yet another important point that is often overlooked. No one can guide their own soul without Allah's permission and favour. Our will to act will never be independent of His decree and grace. Thus, it is imperative for us to turn to Him if we want to succeed, whether in this world or the next.

> "Verily this is no less than a Message to all the Worlds of Beings: for any of you who wills to take the Straight Way. Nor would you ever will unless Allah, the Sustainer of all the worlds, wills to show you that way." (*al-Takwīr*, 27-29)

Sūrah al-Infiṭār

The Main Theme

Anyone who has read the Qur'an and faithfully considered its evidences and vivid descriptions of the Day of Judgement up to this point would have to accept the truth claims it presents; such is the case as long as they are reading the word of Allah with an open mind. The key barrier to guidance is that people's beliefs are not dictated solely by their rational minds, but also by their lowly and sensuous desires. The comforts of this world can be so enjoyable and utility-maximizing that we might never want it to end. Moreover, the sense of control that we exert over our environment can be so addictive that we might produce and achieve worldly gains to keep it for as long as we live. In sum, Allah made this world subservient for us, enjoyable, and peaceful to the extent that we can delude ourselves into believing that this wave of pleasures and amusements will never end and that we will never be held accountable for what we do in this life.

This is one of the main issues of concern that Sūrah al-Infiṭār effectively addresses. It dispels our delusions by reminding us of the terrifying scene of the Day of Resurrection, thereby showcasing to us our humble origins and the lack of control we exerted over the starting point of our own existence, the meticulous accounting and recording of every action that we perform in the temporal world, and the eternal consequences for our deeds. It is the second *sūrah* of a distinguished group that gives us a vivid portrayal of the Day of Resurrection, as described by the Prophet ﷺ, "Whoever wishes to look at the Day of Resurrection, as if he is seeing it with this own eyes, then let him recite 'When the Sun is folded' (*al-Takwīr*), 'When the heaven is cleft asunder' (*al-Infiṭār*), and 'When the heaven is split asunder' (*al-Inshiqāq*)." (al-Tirmidhī)

By closely reading this *sūrah*, we will come to the genuine realization that we are truly in need of Allah for everything, and the more we deny this concrete fact, the worse it will be for us in the next life. For as Allah states, *"It will be the Day when no one shall have the power to do anything for another: for, on that Day, Allah shall keep the entire command to Himself."* (*al-Infiṭār*, 19)

The Context: The Delusion of Mercy

One of the main reasons for the delusion of believing that there will never be a Day of Judgement or any moral consequences for sin is because Allah is extensively forbearing. The basis for this delusion stems from Allah's patience: He does not punish us for a sin immediately, and usually He will not punish us for most sins throughout our entire lives. He postpones His punishment, not because He is incapable or fears us, but in order to give us the maximum time possible to seek forgiveness. This all stems from His infinite generosity, and is not indicative of any weakness.

This beneficent postponement of accountability can lead many of us to make the false assumption that no being or entity is recording what we are doing so long as we hide it from being public. Even worse, we sometimes assume that there will never be a punishment at all for our misdeeds. The more certain we become of this bold and grand delusion, the bolder we will become in challenging His Message and increasing in our level of rebelliousness.

This was the mentality of many of the disbelievers during the time of the Prophet ﷺ. They became so fervent in their opposition to him that they not only tortured and killed his Companions j, but some of them went as far as physically attacking him. Had He wished, Allah could have easily disposed of the Prophet's enemies just as He did with previous rebellious nations. However, He commissioned the Prophet ﷺ as a mercy to humanity, and thus ordered him to patiently persevere the harm inflicted upon him such that his people would be granted the opportunity to rehabilitate themselves and embrace the true faith of Islam. Indeed, some of them did change and embrace Islam, but many of early leaders of the Quraysh did not and ultimately met a humiliating demise. They became prime examples of how delusional disbelievers can become when Allah is generous and forbearing with them. According to Imam al-Baghawī r, this is why Allah revealed part of this *sūrah*, that is, as a result of the attacks meted against the Prophet ﷺ. These *āyāt* were sent down to address al-Aswad ibn Sharīq, who had dared to strike the Prophet ﷺ. Allah did not immediately punish him, but instead revealed, *"O humanity! What has made you delusional about your Lord, the Most Generous?"* (*al-Infiṭār*, 6)

Upon reading the rest of the *sūrah*, we come to the realization that Allah's generosity with us does not in any terms entail that there will never be an account or punishment, for those who refuse to open their eyes to the truth in this life will undoubtedly learn this in the harshest way possible.

The Relationship with Sūrah al-Takwīr

Sūrah al-Infiṭār shares so many literary and thematic parallels with Sūrah al-Takwīr that, for the inexperienced reader, it is quite difficult to tell the difference between them. After all, they begin in similar ways and the subject matter is almost exactly the same.

However, after taking a closer look, we will find that Sūrah al-Infiṭār has many key details that are distinctly different from Sūrah al-Takwīr. And when we combine these distinct details with the ones found in Sūrah al-Takwīr, we will ultimately yield a more comprehensive understanding of all the major themes that Sūrah al-Takwīr entails.

For example, the two chapters give different yet complementary descriptions of how the sky will appear on the Day of Judgement. They both also describe the seas in two different ways. In a similar fashion, while Sūrah al-Takwīr describes the stars, Sūrah al-Infiṭār describes the planets. Furthermore, the mountains are also given two different descriptions.

The same type of complementary style can be discerned when the angels are described. While Sūrah al-Takwīr focuses on how Angel Jibrīl عليه السلام was appointed to the Prophet ﷺ, Sūrah al-Infiṭār concentrates on the Angels appointed to the rest of humanity. Moreover, whereas Sūrah al-Takwīr highlights the character of the Prophet ﷺ and his credibility as an upright figure, we find that Sūrah al-Infiṭār highlights the relationship of people with his message and the consequences found in accepting or rejecting it.

All these thought-provoking comparisons should give us a deep understanding of what to expect on the Day of Resurrection, even down to the most minute of details. It is as if Allah f wants us to be able to imagine this Day as vividly as possible, that is, to the extent that we can see the life of this world as it truly is. For the present world is nothing more than a temporary place for us to manifest who we are and then prepare for the trials of the real permanent world to come.

Thematic Explanation of the Sūrah

A key factor which feeds our delusion of the permanence of the world is the perfection of the ecosystem that Allah has created to support our respective lives. Allah has placed essential components and life-supporting systems in this world to sustain all the fundamental building blocks of life for all of us equally, such as the stars, the sky, the mountains, and the seas. These aforementioned systems work in perfect harmony to create and sustain the environment we need to survive.

The first segment of Sūrah al-Takwīr immediately dispels this delusion of permanence by destroying all those fundamental components such that we will reevaluate everything we initially assumed we knew about our lives in this world and the one to come:

> "When the sky is shattered to pieces, and the bright stars are strewn asunder, and the seas explode in flames beyond their bounds, and deep graves turned flung out, then every soul shall know what they send ahead and left undone behind." (*al-Takwīr*, 1-5)

Although this aforementioned warning of impending doom and destruction should be sufficient to strike the fear of God in any sincere and conscious person, Allah f is aware that many of us are excessively steeped in the comforts of His provisions and do not make accurate long-term projections that consider the other world; our delusions are severe to the extent that we might falsely assume that even if Allah resurrected us, He would still treat us as well or even better than He is currently treating us in this world, regardless of whether or not we abide by His commandments. Such delusional people are like the arrogant man described in Sūrah al-Kahf, "*When, having thus wronged his soul, he entered his garden and said: 'I do not think that this garden will ever perish! Nor do I believe that the Hour of Judgement will ever come. And even if I am returned to my Lord, I will surely find even a better place than this.'*" (*al-Kahf*, 35-36) As a result, Allah dedicates the next part of the *sūrah* to nullify these grave misconceptions. His generosity and beneficence towards us comes with a strong responsibility to follow the truth, for He has created mortal beings in order to test them and assess how well they comply with His divine commandments.

> "O ever-forgetful Man: What has deluded you about your magnanimous noble Lord? Who created you, then formed you perfect, then balanced you evenly out moulding you in whatever form He willed? By no means: Indeed you cry lies to the very Reckoning; while over you are those keeping close watch. Noble angels who record in writing. Who know everything you do." (*al-Infiṭār*, 6-12)

To conclude, Allah promises us that the indiscriminate generosity that He extends to us now is only for this temporary world. Conversely, the pleasures and blessings of the Hereafter are reserved only for those who were virtuous in this life. As for the misguided ones who deluded themselves into thinking that they could reject the truth and shamelessly disobey Allah in this world, they will face eternally dreadful consequences in the permanent realm. They will realize in the next life that all the powers and abilities that Allah gave them have been stripped away without any prior warning, and they will have no choice but to accept the eternal judgement of a painful torment from Allah.

> "Verily, those devoted to Him with all works of good are in bliss. And verily the wicked are in a raging fire; roasting in it on the Day of Reckoning. And they shall never be able to escape from it. What will make you realize what Judgement Day is? And more dire yet, what will make you realize what Judgement Day is? It will be the Day when no one shall have the power to do anything for another. And the command that Day is Allah's." (*al-Infiṭār*, 13-19)

Sūrah al-Muṭaffifīn

The Main Theme

When Allah speaks of criminals and wrongdoers in the Qur'an, our minds often envision people who have done outstandingly egregious acts, such as murder. We assume that the crimes that lead people to Hell have to be shockingly wrong according to our own society-set standards in order for the eternal punishment of Jahannam to be justified. Seemingly small violations and wrongs that are deemed culturally acceptable in modern times might be overlooked by the limited and politically-shaped courts of this world because they are too nuanced and hard to prove. However, on the Day of Judgement those seemingly marginal yet damaging transgressions might mean the difference between a person going to Heaven or Hell.

This is where Sūrah al-Muṭaffifīn enters the picture and challenges the dominant discourse in a paradigm-shifting manner. In this *sūrah*, we learn that a person who spends their life manipulating and cheating people in even the smallest of ways can be the worst kind of criminal in the sight of Allah. Although they might assume that their victims are too naive and innocent to defend themselves from being cheated out of their hard-earned wealth and precious resources, Allah spends this entire *sūrah* by exposing their evil doings and thoughts, and shows us how, in reality, these criminals are slowly cheating themselves into an eternal life of misery and pain.

In contrast, we also learn in this beautiful *sūrah* that those virtuous people who were cheated, manipulated, and mocked might in fact lose some of the small comforts of this world. But in the end, they will ultimately find that they were earning far greater comforts all along, and come to the realization that this trade-off was worth all the indignities that they suffered at the hands of the petty criminals in this life. Once again, we learn that everything in this world is ultimately valued not by the standards of this life, but by the eternal rewards and consequences that they entail in the long run. Sūrah al-Muṭaffifīn is a warning and reminder of this stark reality, and we should thus act accordingly.

The Context: Petty Crimes with Major Consequences

When the Prophet Muhammad ﷺ migrated to Madina, he faced the pressing task of changing negative cultural habits that had been developed over the centuries in the city's milieu. Many of these abysmal habits were concentrated in the business culture of Madina, which was predicated on a number of problematic financial instruments. The economic world of Madina was heavily influenced by an oppressive interest-based economy that was largely run by a Jewish clan known as the Banū Qaynuqāᶜ. Interest rates were extremely high and any notion of religious consciousness was hollow and shallow. This ultimately caused the marketplace to become a place of various and nuanced forms of fraud, such that everyone was vying to gain an unfair advantage in even the smallest of business deals.

According to al-Quraẓī, as cited in al-Wāḥidī's *Asbāb al-Nuzūl*, there were a myriad of amoral business practices that the Prophet ﷺ encountered. Some corrupt factions turned transactions into gambling, whereby they would assign ownership through the means of throwing a pebble on a specific piece of merchandise (*munābadhah*) without stipulating any terms or agreeing on a contract. Another arbitrary practice involved having a buyer purchase a form of merchandise by blindly touching it (*mulāmasah*). Others engaged in a nefarious form of short selling by trading an overpriced product through financing and then later buying back the product for a small price, while still being owed the original amount from the buyer (*mukhāṭarah*). To address these outstanding financial ills, Allah revealed, *"Woe to the defrauders."* (*al-Muṭaffifīn*, 1) According to al-Suddī, in the pre-Islamic setting there was even a man who had one doctored scale he would use for selling products and another doctored scale he would use to buy products, thereby always gaining an unfair advantage in every transaction they undertook.

These are the types of fraudulent practices that were addressed in Sūrah al-Muṭaffifīn. In addition to the revelation of this *sūrah*, the Prophet ﷺ ordered the Muslims to buy their own land so they could create their own marketplace that was governed by fair practices and regulated by divine Islamic laws. By creating their own distinct economic sphere, the Muslims became liberated from the oppressive environment of the old marketplace of the Banū Qaynuqāʿ clan; they attained financial independence, which allowed the Muslim economy to flourish and be driven by the keen, experienced Qurayshī Muslim merchants who had newly migrated from Makkah. Moreover, it created an outlet and hub for righteous people to infuse their spiritual values in business practices and avoid the torments that they were warned about in Sūrah al-Muṭaffifīn.

The Relationship with Sūrah al-Infiṭār

As previously noted in the study of Sūrah al-Infiṭār, Allah f does *not* overlook any violations against His Prophet ﷺ, the believers, or any innocent victims, for He will exact His retribution upon the criminals and wrongdoers through His infinite justice. However, one might believe that in His warnings Allah is only addressing the worst of people, such as Abū Jahl or al-Walīd ibn Mughīrah, who exerted the most radical of efforts to oppose the Prophet ﷺ.

In this context, one can consider the statement of Allah in Sūrah al-Infiṭār, *"By no means: Indeed you cry lies to the very Reckoning; while over you are those keeping close watch. Noble angels who record in writing. Who know everything you do."* (*al-Infiṭār*, 9-12) Here, Allah was not simply speaking of how the major violations would be recorded and taken to account in the Hereafter, but was also alluding to the nuanced violations that one does regularly, which,over time, accumulate to a mountain of sin. We will be questioned about all the resources and advantages that Allah allotted to us in this life and how we used them, especially if we employed them to defraud others of the provisions that Allah provided them. Sūrah al-Muṭaffifīn very clearly demonstrates this point.

In addition, when Allah stated in Sūrah al-Infiṭār, *"O ever-forgetful Man: What has deluded you about your magnanimous noble Lord?"* (*al-Infiṭār*, 6), He was dispelling the notion that His non-immediate issuance of a punishment is a reason to think that we will get away with crimes, even if they appear marginal or relatively insignificant. He does not describe specific examples of delusional people who fit this description in that *sūrah*, but He does so in Sūrah al-Muṭaffifīn from the very first *āyah*.

Thematic Explanation of the Sūrah

This is the first *sūrah* in the Qur'an that begins with the term *wayl* (lit. woe). Interestingly, there are only two chapters in the Qur'an that begin with this stern word of dispraise, with both of them relating to people who are obsessed with financial gain. In Sūrah al-Humazah, Allah says, "*Woe to every slanderer and defamer, who amasses wealth greedily and counts it repeatedly.*" (*al-Humazah*, 1-2)

The theme that we derive from the latter verse is that for the most part, people largely underestimate the danger of having an unhealthy relationship with wealth. Of particular concern is the fact that the underlying cause of greed and petty fraud is disbelief in the Last Day, which many people fail to note. Moreover, because these deceptive people rob in small amounts, they seldom come to the realization that this is more destructive to their eternal destiny than what might meet the eye. Allah warns them emphatically in this Quranic chapter to alert them to the danger that is in store for them if they continue to underestimate the severity of their crime.

> "Woe to the slightest stinters in weight or measure: Those who take full measure [when they buy] from people, but when they give by measure or by weight to others, they give less than due. Do they not think that they will be raised to life again, for a tremendous Day? The Day all people will stand in judgement before the Lord of all Worlds of Beings? By no means! Verily the record of the godlessly wicked shall be written in Sijjīn. And what will make you realize what Sijjīn is? This is a written book of hell. Woe on that Day to the deniers; who deny the Day of Judgement! None denies it except every godless transgressor steeped in sin. Who, when Our revelations are recited to him, says: 'These are make-believe tales written by the ancient peoples.'" (*al-Muṭaffifīn*, 1-13)

In this moving and powerful passage, Allah clarifies to us the reason for this disbelief: those consistent sins slowly corrode the heart of the swindlers to the point that they will be veiled from His mercy. When they are veiled from divine mercy, it logically follows that Hell is the only destiny for them. For such depraved individuals did not believe that they would be taken to task for all the small yet incremental violations they dared to make with the lawful wealth of people. They forgot that Allah takes the rights of wealth seriously, and that vengeance will be exacted for every penny that is intentionally usurped under false grounds or dubious means. Meanwhile, Allah praises the victims of these fraudsters who persevered with the ethic of beautiful patience and remained vigilant of the Reckoning. Such morally conscious individuals – who exercised the utmost degree of caution with other people's wealth – will gain tremendous profits in the life to come.

> "Nay, but their hearts are corroded by all [the evil] that they used to commit. Undoubtedly, they will be sealed off from their Lord on that Day. And then, behold, they shall enter the blazing fire and be told: 'This is what you used to deny.' Nay, those devoted to their Lord with all works of good is in ʿIlliyyīn. And what will explain to you what the ʿIlliyyīn is? This is a written book, witnessed by those nearest to Allah." (*al-Muṭaffifīn*, 14-21)

With his perfect and infinite knowledge, Allah recognizes that many people have a natural obsession with material possessions, which causes them to have a lack of control and continue to seek ways to gain an unfair relative advantage. Moreover, Allah also wants to give hope to the people who are unwearyingly persevering with all the oppression and indignities that they have faced at the hands of the disbelievers. Hence, He reminds them that their difficulties will be rewarded with such great pleasures that they will look forward to accepting even more worldly sacrifices in order to gain the maximum rewards.

> "Surely those devoted to their Lord with all works of good will be in bliss, reclining on majestic raised canopied couches, joyously gazing. You will recognize on their faces the radiant joy of bliss. They are served exquisitely pure delicious sealed wine, and its seal

is the finest musk. Those who wish to excel above others, let them endeavour to excel in this. And it is mixed with lofty Tasnīm: a spring from which those nearest to Allah will drink." (*al-Muṭaffifīn*, 22-28)

One can deduce that after highlighting the punishment of the sinners and the reward of the virtuous and believing servants, Allah consoles the hearts of the believers by showing them that although the criminals are laughing at them in this life, the believers will certainly have the last laugh for all of eternity in the next world. Furthermore, the emotional pain of the mockery and humiliation they were forced to undergo will add even more rewards for them in a twofold fashion. For in Paradise, they will be given their turn to laugh at their opponents when they observe them suffering in Hell, thereby adding more pleasure to the virtuous for seeing what they were saved from. In addition, the psychological torment of regret for the people of Hell will be increased when they realize all the pleasures they are missing.

"Those who committed crimes used to laugh at those who believed. And they mock them with gesturing eyes and winks as they passed them by. And muse over these exploits upon returning to their own people. And when they saw the faithful, they would say, 'These miserable souls are completely lost,' even though they were not sent to watch over them. So today the believers will be laughing at the disbelievers, as they sit on majestic raised canopied couches, gazing on. The believers will be asked, 'Have the disbelievers not been paid back for what they used to do?'" (*al-Muṭaffifīn*, 29-36)

Sūrah al-Inshiqāq

The Main Theme

This is the last of the three unique *sūrahs* concerning which the Prophet ﷺ said, "Whoever wishes to look at the Day of Resurrection, as if he is seeing it with this own eyes, then let him recite 'When the Sun is folded' (*al-Takwīr*), 'When the heaven is cleft asunder' (*al-Infiṭār*), and 'When the heaven is split asunder' (*al-Inshiqāq*)." (al-Tirmidhī)

In this *sūrah*, Allah f vividly illustrates how hope and heedlessness play out in this world and the next. While hope consists of performing the necessary hard work early on while patiently expecting a great payoff in the future, heedlessness and disobedience of the Divine causes a person to exceed the religious norms of moderation; this in turn leads them to seek the comforts in this world while actively disregarding the dreadful consequences that await in the future.

Sūrah al-Inshiqāq serves as a solemn reminder that members of humanity will be divided into only two groups on the Day of Judgement. These two groups are defined by the records that they built and drafted for themselves in this world. We have been previously warned in several *sūrahs* about the records that are actively being written, retained, and updated throughout our time in this life. Now, within the confines of this *sūrah,* Allah shows us how those records will be brought forth and presented on the Day of Judgement.

The Context: The Pursuit of Happiness

When the Prophet ﷺ began preaching the message of monotheism in Mecca, the believers often found themselves under constant stress and pressure from the disbelievers. Some would be physically battered, others would be starved, the families of another group would be torn apart and banished from their tribes, and yet another segment among them would be tortured to death and displayed in public. All of the aforementioned groups experienced public humiliation and embarrassment by being publicly insulted, socially shunned, and closely monitored. Throughout this ordeal, the believers would find the disbelievers indulging in a variety of comforts with their families, laughing with each other and entertaining themselves with the luxuries of total freedom and unparalleled social status. To the untrained eye, it might have appeared that Allah had abandoned His believers based on the emotional and social turmoil that He allowed them to go through and favoured the disbelievers by allotting them ease and comforts in this world.

Allah revealed Sūrah al-Inshiqāq during these pressing and difficult times to elucidate the wisdom of these trials through a new and enlightening perspective. The life of this world is is nothing more than a series of challenging yet purifying difficulties that we are supposed to face before returning to Allah. Our Creator and Sustainer further demonstrates that the tribulations and sadness that the believers were facing during this most demanding time were quite paradoxically a means of preparing for unimaginable happiness, while the current state of enjoyment that the disbelievers experience in the worldly realm is all the comfort they will ever have, for they will face a life of eternal depression and regret in the next world.

The Relationship With Sūrah al-Muṭaffifīn

In Sūrah al-Muṭaffifīn, Allah provides us a telling sign of how the people of Hell behave in this world when they entertain themselves by mocking the believers, *"And [they] muse over these exploits upon returning to their own people."* (*al-Muṭaffifīn*, 32)

Anticipating that the reader likely assumed that this detail would be overlooked on the Day of Judgement, Allah further notes to us in Sūrah al-Inshiqāq that even this detailed element of sin will bear its equal consequence on the Day of Judgement, *"Behold, [in his earthly life] he lived joyfully among people of his own kind. Behold, he never thought that he would have to return [to God]."* (*al-Inshiqāq*, 13-14)

Moreover, one of the major themes found in Sūrah al-Muṭaffifīn that the names and contents of the record books for the virtuous and the criminals will be publicized in the Hereafter. This can be deduced from the verses, "*By no means! Verily the record of the godlessly wicked shall be written in Sijjīn*" (*al-Muṭaffifīn*, 7) and, "*Nay, those devoted to their Lord with all works of good is in ʿIlliyyīn.*" (*al-Muṭaffifīn*, 18) However, we remain uninformed of what exactly happens to these books, that is, until we turn to and peruse Sūrah al-Inshiqāq.

Lastly, in Sūrah al-Muṭaffifīn Allah rhetorically asks why people ignore His warnings and fail to anticipate the Day of Judgement, "*Do they not think that they will be raised to life again, for a tremendous Day? The Day all people will stand in judgement before the Lord of all Worlds of Beings?*" (*al-Muṭaffifīn*, 4-6) As such, Allah emphatically declares to humanity that the difficulties of the Day must be a matter of primary importance in their minds, "*O humanity! Indeed, you are labouring restlessly towards your Lord, and will meet the consequences.*" (*al-Muṭaffifīn*, 6) It is as if Allah is sending a message repeatedly from beyond the heavens that we can and should not underestimate the hardships and horrors that people will face on the Day of Resurrection. The ones who pay heed to this warning the most will have the easiest Reckoning on that Day.

Thematic Explanation of the Sūrah

This *sūrah* commences by introducing new details regarding the Day of Resurrection. In previous *sūrahs*, Allah described the unparalleled and unprecedented cosmic events of the Day as well. But on this occasion, He emphasizes that these events happen due to the irresistible force of His Will, and it sets the tone for us to understand how uncontrollable every detail of our situation will be. These shocking facts prepare us for the unimaginable difficulties that we will be forced to experience.

> "When heaven will split asunder, obeying its Lord as it must. When the earth will be drawn taut stretched out, and throws up what is in it, and voids itself convulsively empty, while obeying its Lord as it must. O humanity! Indeed, you are toiling your trouble-scarred way towards your Lord, and will inevitably meet Him." (*al-Muṭaffifīn*, 1-6)

Upon ensuring that we appreciate how grave this Day is, Allah introduces us to its decisive grand finale. After spending thousands of years worth of trials during that fateful Day, we will finally meet Allah and will see the results of what we have done in our respective lives, whereby we will have no choice but to accept the deeds we committed. We will also find that our own bodies will move and testify regarding our actions without any input in our part. This should not be a matter of surprise, as all our limbs are under Allah's control just as the sky and the Earth function in accordance with His will. Thus, we will receive our records according to the nature of our deeds: if we were upright and blessed with divine guidance in this life and bore the difficulties of following it, we will reflexively receive our records with our right hands and be given an easy reckoning. In stark contrast, the ones who shunned the dictates of divine guidance in this world and turned their backs to it will reflexively receive their records behind their backs, which will signify their impending doom. At that very moment, those who had been looking forward to their reward on this Day will finally find that all their worldly sacrifices were profitable, while those who opted for the comforts of this temporal world over the next life will go as far as regretting that they had even existed in the first place.

> "Then he who will be given his Book of deeds in his right hand, shall have a quick and easy reckoning, and he will turn to his people rejoicing! But he who will be given his book of deeds from behind his back, he shall plead ceaselessly for destruction to end him, and will be roasted in a raging blaze. Truly he had always been with his family and kin in happiness. Verily he was sure he would never meet anything else beyond that. Indeed he would! Truly his Lord was ever watchful of him." (*al-Inshiqāq*, 7-15)

Allah concludes this *sūrah* by urging us to take this reminder and warning with the utmost seriousness. He appeals to us to simply look at the obvious signs of the sky that is situated above us, and appreciate the magnificent changes that occur to it everyday. The awesome cosmos which surround us serve as an evidence that we were created for a noble purpose. Such a discovery should elicit the following response: "*...You* *have not created all of this without purpose. Glory be to You! Protect us from the torment of the Fire."* (*Āl 'Imrān*, 191) Allah also shows us how astonished we should be of a person who – when being promised of horrors that are terrifying enough to make a person wish they were dust – would ignore all the intuitive evidence of its occurrence and wait until the Day of Reckoning to find out if it is true. Anyone who is rebellious to that degree and insistent on sin will have no one to blame but themselves when they see the dreadful consequences to come.

> "Then no, I need not even swear by the vanishing last light of sunset, and by the night and all that it enshroudeth, and the Moon when it waxes full brilliant: Verily all of you shall have to ride out one direr stage after another! So how can they possibly not believe, and when the Qur'an is recited to them, do not prostrate? Rather, those who disbelieve cry lies. Yet, God has full knowledge of what they conceal. So give them good news of a painful punishment; except those who embrace the true faith and do good deeds; for them there will be a never ending reward." (*al-Inshiqāq*, 25)

Sūrah al-Burūj

The Main Theme

When believers are abused at the hands of the disbelievers simply due to following the guidance of Allah, this can cause both parties to raise questions. On the one hand, the disbelievers will taunt the believers by asking them why Allah allows them to punish the believers so cavalierly. The question being posed here is quite obvious: if the believers follow the true Creator, why is He not stopping us from doing this to you?

On the other hand, during their painful and pressing ordeal, the believers might also begin to ask themselves similar questions, such as "When will Allah's help arrive?" Other queries might also be brought up, like "Has Allah abandoned me?", "Have I done something wrong?", and "How can this happen to me when I am on the truth?"

Sūrah al-Burūj addresses the painful internal doubts of the believers and the bold and wicked plots of the disbelievers. In it, we learn that Allah's control is ever-present; His divine justice is well-proven throughout every epoch of history, and it operates according to His infinite wisdom and the time that He Himself chooses. Any believer who suffers when following the true message of guidance can console themselves with this *sūrah* and know with full certainty that they are, in fact, following the same path of righteousness as those before them in human history, and that they are in the process of earning the same rewards accrued by their righteous predecessors, who made similar or even greater sacrifices. As for the disbelievers who oppress and unjustly wrong them, they will suffer the same fate as the disbelievers who preceded them in history, and one does not need to look that far in the past to see examples of their worldly demise.

The Context: The Arc of Justice

During the Meccan period, the Companions of the Prophet ﷺ were not in a position – nor given divine permission – to defend themselves or resist the oppression of the Quraysh. This single fact is what allowed the leaders of the Quraysh to sadistically have their way with the Muslims from within their own clans. Slaves who had embraced Islam, such as Bilāl ibn Rabāḥ h, were severely tortured by being chained and fettered, dragged over hot sand and sharp rocks in the blazing heat of the desert, lashed in quick succession, and smothered with large boulders to the point that their tongues would unconsciously come out of their mouths as they gasped for air. The poor among the believers, like the family of ʿAmmār ibn Yāsir h, were tortured together, deprived of any food or water, whipped, and maimed; when they still held strong on their belief, Abū Jahl mercilessly killed ʿAmmār's mother and father in front of him, blaming ʿAmmār for the fatal fate of his parents. In addition, there were other steadfast believers such as Khabbāb h, who was tortured by his female owner in a myriad of sadistic ways. His naked body would be placed on a layer of steel armour and left out in the Sun on the hottest days of the summer, such that his skin would slowly burn on the burning metal. On other occasions, she would stoke a fire beneath a metal rod until it became red-hot and then place it on his head. During the ordeal, Khabbāb h would be dragged over heaps of scorching coals until the fat and blood would sizzle off of his back. To make matters worse, all these horrifying crimes would be done in plain sight for the world to see.

It was during this very disturbing and horrifying context that Sūrah al-Burūj was revealed. Allah reminded the steadfast Companions j of the tyrannical nations before them who had done much worse to the believers. He thus reminded them of the rewards of those who remained steadfast, and the punishment of those who oppressed them. This was a crucial *sūrah* for the believers to recite and remember during some of the most difficult and critical times in Islamic history.

The Relationship with Sūrah al-Inshiqāq

Sūrah al-Inshiqāq perfectly complements Sūrah al-Burūj in several ways. When Allah says in the former, *"O humanity! Indeed, you are toiling your trouble-scarred way towards your Lord, and will inevitably meet Him"* (*al-Inshiqāq*, 5), He follows this promise with real world examples of people who went through suffering in Sūrah al-Burūj, showing them that their suffering will not be in vain. This series of verses also served as a reminder that everything is being carefully recorded and will be duly rewarded. This is why people of piety like Khabbāb h became alarmed later in life when Islam became a dominant force, spread exponentially, and wealth began to increase among the Muslims. He would often worry that Allah might be compensating them in this world and it would ultimately lessen the rewards of their sacrifices in the Hereafter.

Moreover, in Sūrah al-Inshiqāq we come across *āyāt* that taunt the disbelievers such as the following: *"So give them good news of a painful punishment; except those who embrace the true faith and do good deeds; for them there will be a never ending reward."* (*al-Inshiqāq*, 24-25) The warning ingrained in this verse was refreshing news to the believers, who were suffering at the hands of the likes of Abū Jahl and Umayyah, who were among the most hostile enemies of Islam. Sūrah al-Burūj builds on this message by sharing well-known accounts of tyrannical groups who fit the same description and describing how Allah fulfilled His threats to them. These include the people of the Ditch, Firʿawn, and Thamūd. By reading this chapter, the Companions would have noted that Allah was warning the leaders of Quraysh that they would meet the same dreadful end of these aforementioned groups.

Thematic Explanation of the Sūrah

Allah commences the *sūrah* by swearing upon the stars or the Angels, depending on which exegetical interpretation is adopted. Regardless of which opinion is preferred, an overarching theme can be discerned, since both of these created beings share two things in common. They both give us direction and guidance, while also giving us a sense of being watched by a Higher Power. If we reflect upon these two key features, we will realize that what is currently unfolding on the Earth is being displayed in full view of the celestial sphere of the heavens. But on the Day that this show ends, there will certainly be Hell for those who were on the wrong side of history, such as the People of the Ditch.

> "By the Sky with many tremendous constellations, and by the final promised Day, and by shocked Eyewitnesses, and what shall be appallingly Beheld: slain be those of the long-trenched pit! The fiery blaze kept mounted high with fuel. As they were seated long presiding over it; seeing with their own eyes what they were doing to the believers. While they seethed so fiercely against them for nothing but their believing in Allah, the Invincible, the All-Laudable; Who possesses the kingdom of the heavens and the earth. And Allah is all-present witness over every single thing!" (*al-Burūj*, 1-9)

In this latter segment, Allah declares that He is the Invincible and the All-Laudable (i.e. Praiseworthy). Hence, Allah dedicated the next passage of the *sūrah* to illustrating how these attributes are actually manifested in the concrete realm. Those who oppose Allah will find out why He is Invincible, and those who patiently persevere for the sake of Allah will eventually find every reason to praise Him the moment they see the rewards that are in store for them.

> "Those who persecute the believing men and believing women and do never repent, no matter how long after, shall receive the punishment of Hell, wherein they shall have the punishment of the raging fire. Lo! those who believe and work righteous deeds, theirs will be lush groves of Paradise underneath which rivers flow. That is the mighty undying triumph." (*al-Burūj*, 10-11)

Most of our doubts about Allah's justice and rewards stems from our lack of knowledge of His attributes. To address this gap, Allah reminds both disbelievers and believers of Who He is and what He is capable of. The following *āyāt* are meant for deep contemplation and continuous reflection in all contexts and circumstances. Upon doing so, we will be able to keep all lifelong states and episodes within a proper framework and perspective.

"Indeed, the crushing grip of your Lord is severe. Lo! He alone originates, then brings back again. And He alone is truly-forgiving, the Ever Tenderly Loving-kind. The Incomparably Noble Possessor of the very Throne. Forever the Doer of all He wills." (*al-Burūj*, (*al-Burūj*, 12-16)

Yet, Allah does not stop at simply making the aforementioned claim. Rather, He follows His claims with ample and convincing proof from the past great nations. In fact, Allah specifically cites historical evidence that is physically verifiable and historically irrefutable: Firʿawn and the people of Thamūd. Firʿawn's humiliating legacy physically exists for anyone to see, and the story of his downfall is unanimously agreed upon by all Abrahamic traditions. Allah informs us that He specifically preserved Pharaoh's body with the very purpose of proving His promise to all people who come after him, *"We shall save your lifeless body this day, as a mighty sign of an example made for whoever comes after you. And indeed, many among mankind are utterly heedless of Our momentous signs!"* (*Yūnus*, 92) Similarly, Allah invokes a regionally relevant piece of evidence with the people of Thamūd, because He knew that the Arabs frequently passed by the mountains that they were destroyed in. These stories are just as famous and widely distributed as the massacre of the People of the Ditch, who existed one generation before the Prophet Muhammad ﷺ, and the Quraysh knew well the untimely demise of the people from that era.

Hence, Allah concludes this noble chapter by bringing these stories to the forefront of the minds of the Quraysh such that they could reflect on the outcome of their deeds and know what kind of retribution awaits them. That way, they could realize that no matter the efforts that they expend, the message of the Qur'an will never be destroyed.

"Have you not heard the story of the forces, of Pharaoh, and of [the tribe of] Thamūd? Yet the disbelievers persist in denial. But Allah encompasses them from all sides. Nay this is a Glorious Qur'an, inscribed on an Imperishable Tablet." (*al-Burūj*, 17-22)

Sūrah al-Ṭāriq

The Main Theme

A notable factor that emboldens the rebelliousness of people against Allah is their acute unawareness of their own inherent fragility, as well as their failure to estimate Allah's power over them. These false notions are exposed and dismantled in Sūrah al-Ṭāriq, where Allah's power over the heavens, His power over the Earth, and even His control over every stage of our development is highlighted.

When Allah warns us that the Day of Judgement is a matter of certainty and that the enemies of the Message will never succeed in their evil plots, we will have these signs as a frame of reference of the depth of Allah's power and know how easily these threats can be manifested.

The Context: A Wake Up Call

Initially, the Prophet ﷺ mainly preached the message of Islam to his tribe, the Quraysh. Members of the latter confederation were pagans who did not believe in the Day of Resurrection, nor did they place much faith in unseen forces; hence, they made physical idols and worshipped them. This faith and dependance on material objects proved to be a difficult challenge to the Prophet ﷺ, and he had to rely heavily on physical evidences and naturally intuitive arguments to convince his people of the Message of the unseen world.

Consequently, when the Prophet ﷺ faced difficulties with his nation and came to an impasse, he was in urgent need of reinforcement to lift his spirits. Subsequently, Allah sent new signs to him through the Qur'an that confounded the Quraysh into a state of silence and awe. In this context, Sūrah al-Ṭāriq was one of those chapters that had this powerful effect. Specifically, it reminded these heedless idol worshippers of the lofty and absolute power of Allah, the small-mindedness of their belief in destructible idols, and transparent plots against the Prophet ﷺ.

This particular chapter was revealed about Abū Ṭālib. He once went to visit the Prophet ﷺ, who offered him bread and milk. As Abū Ṭālib was sitting and eating, a meteor fell, filling all of their surroundings with a blazing fire. Abū Ṭālib was shocked and horrified with this sight. He asked: "What on Earth can this be?" The Prophet ﷺ said: "This is a meteor that was thrown, and it is one of the signs of Allah." Abū Ṭālib was amazed to hear this response from him, and so Allah f revealed these verses.

Relationship with Sūrah al-Burūj

In Sūrah al-Burūj, Allah declares He will torment the enemies of the believers, and He cites historical proof as iron-clad evidence to back His promise. But in Sūrah al-Ṭāriq, Allah supplements this historical foundation with biological evidence of our own origins, thereby demonstrating to us the absolute control that He has in our beginning and – as a logical corollary – our ending.

In Sūrah al-Burūj, Allah directs us to look at the constellations in the sky, *"By the Sky with many tremendous constellations,"* (*al-Burūj*, 1). Yet, in Sūrah al-Ṭāriq, He adds to this theme by telling us to look even more narrowly to the individual star, showcasing to us His power over the individual and the collective realms.

In Sūrah al-Burūj, Allah declares His power to reproduce all things: *"Lo! He alone originates, then brings back again."* (*al-Burūj*, 13) It is in Sūrah al-Ṭāriq, however, where Allah bolsters this claim with specific evidence by pointing to the sky and the Earth as concrete demonstrations of this power, *"By the sky with its recurring cycles of rain, and the earth, bursting forth with plants!"* (*al-Ṭāriq*, 11-12)

Just as Sūrahs al-Takwīr and al-Infiṭār complement each other throughout, in a parallel fashion Sūrahs al-Burūj and at-Tariq augment each other and function as companion chapters, for whereas Sūrah al-Burūj provides the initial warning against the disbelievers, Sūrah al-Ṭāriq reinforces it with abundant evidence.

Thematic Explanation of the Sūrah

Allah commences this chapter by swearing on the *ṭāriq*, a term which can have a myriad of denotations. In a general sense, it implies any being or thing - whether observable or unseen - that exerts efforts to make a sound, like a knock at the door, or footsteps on the road at night. Allah specifies the meaning of this base term by mentioning the star whose stunning light pierces through the night. Allah swears by this star because it constitutes tangible evidence of other forces existing around us that we might be temporarily unaware of, but nonetheless have a powerful impact on our lives. And they will reveal our innermost secrets, just as this shining star is rendered manifest in the night.

> "By the Sky, and the Nightcomer! And what may teach you what is the Nightcomer? The ascendant star of dark piercing brightness! Nor is there any soul, but has a watcher over it who misses nothing." (*al-Ṭāriq*, 4)

Many people could question the relevance of having a record of deeds in the first place, since they oftentimes forget the importance of their creation and how much value has been placed in their role and status as a steward in this world. Allah directly addresses this very topic by reminding us to reflect and contemplate upon our origins in order to understand our future. If we appreciate how Allah has transformed us from virtual nothingnesses to something so sophisticated and morally conscious, it would be relatively easy to accept the fact that it was done for a divine purpose, which ultimately calls for an accounting that is equal to its importance.

> "Let man consider from what he is created! He was created from an out-pulsing worthless fluid, that issues from between back and breastbones: Verily, He is well able to bring him back again. On a day when the most secret thoughts and deeds shall be brought openly out and tried. Then one will have neither strength nor any ally." (*al-Ṭāriq*, 5-10)

In addition to referencing our origins, Allah reiterates the inevitability of our own Resurrection by citing evidence from both the sky above us and the ground below us to demonstrate the futility of anyone attempting to oppose their destiny. The wretched ones who plot and scheme against the Message will be doing nothing but taking a futile respite to prepare their own bed of torment in Hell. And Allah consoles the believers by declaring that their time of eternal bliss is coming. So let us be patient with Allah’s justice and demonstrate our full trust in His eternal justice.

> “By the sky with its recurring cycles of rain, and the earth, bursting forth with plants; verily it is a Word that is decisively final! And it is not to be taken lightly. They are certainly devising evil plans, and I, too, am plotting a scheme. Let, then, the deniers of the truth have their will: let them have their will for a little while!” (*al-Ṭāriq*, 11-17)

Sūrah al-A'lā

The Main Theme

When scholars and theologians attempt to determine who the Creator of the universe is, they often overlook a fundamental question, which could be rendered in the following way: "Who is actually making the claim that they are the creator?" Now, it is true that some people in history have made the claim that they themselves, the idols that they make, or some celestial bodies such as the Sun created or influenced human beings. Nevertheless, it will be hard to find anyone who claims that they created the entire universe and everything in it. The reason why this is an important question is because people – and all idols – that are worshipped never actually make the claim in the first place, and consequently there is no reason to even look in those directions to find the Creator. In the Qur'an, however, Allah f makes this claim throughout in an explicit and forthright manner.

While many of the previous *sūrahs* focused on the description of the Day of Judgement, the virtues of the Prophet,ﷺ and the watchful eye of the Angels, Sūrah al-Aʿlā focuses heavily on the attributes and favours of Allah. As we have already noted in the Thematic Explanation of Sūrah al-Naba', He proves His Lordship by providing iron-clad evidence of how 1) He creates, which is explained through the term *al-ījād* (الإيجاد), 2) prepares the universe for us, a notion captured through the term *al-iʿdād* (الإعداد), and 3) sustains our life, a concept exemplified through the Arabic phrase *al-imdād* (الإمداد).

Moreover, in Sūrah al-Aʿlā, Allah goes further by demonstrating that He is not simply the Lord of our external bodies and environment, but He is also the Lord and Sustainer of our souls and afterlife. He effectively establishes this latter point by introducing two new themes in this Quranic chapter: 1) He is the One Who delivers moral guidance, which is exemplified with the term *al-irshād* (الإرشاد), and 2) He is the One Who provides the ultimate reward for following that guidance, which is known as *al-inʿām* (الإنعام). By effectively internalizing these two concepts, we can establish that His Lordship over us is perfect and complete, since He is the One Who sustains our existence and determines our eternal destiny. There is no higher blessing than having a Lord Who showers us with His favour and grace in every conceivable way. Hence, Allah instructs us to glorify Him by revealing the verse: *"Glorify in utter greatness the Name of your Lord Most High."* (*al-Aʿlā*, 1)

The Context: Establishing the Legacy of Ibrāhīm عليه السلام

During the Days of Ignorance, the people of Mecca had corrupted the monotheistic religion of their forefather, Ibrāhīm عليه السلام. Ibrāhīm and his son Ismāʿīl عليه السلام – both of whom were non-Arabs – rebuilt the Kaʿbah as the original house of prayer for worshipping Allah alone. Thereafter, for several centuries the Arabized descendants of Ismāʿīl عليه السلام (who were known as the Adnanites) ruled Mecca with the support of the ancestral Arab tribe of Jurhum. Within that joint setting, they worshipped Allah alone, and the Prophets and Messengers عليهم السلام from around the world throughout history migrated to Mecca to perform Hajj to glorify Allah as the one true God. However, about 200 years before the birth of the Prophet ﷺ, the Khuzāʿah, another ancestral Arab tribe – of non-Abrahamic and pagan origin – ousted the Jurhum and Adnanites (i.e. Quraysh) and took control of Mecca for several hundred years, and it was the latter who began introducing idols to the Kaʿbah. From that point onward, every Arab pagan tribe in the Arabian Peninsula vied to introduce their own idols, until there were eventually 360 idols in the Kaʿbah, and the Hajj rituals became thoroughly infused with paganism.

By the time the Quraysh returned and ousted the Khuzāʿah centuries later, the idols were well established in Mecca with a burgeoning economy revolving around it. Although some members of the Quraysh remained devoted to the primal true faith of Ibrāhīm عليه السلام, they only constituted a minority group, which would be known as the Ḥunafā' (sing. Ḥanīf).

This is the very setting that the Prophet ﷺ encountered when he commenced his mission to spread the message of the Qur'an. It was imperative for him to first reestablish the original and pure religion of monotheism – whose foundations were set by Ibrāhīm ﵇ – in the minds of the ancestral pagan Arabs in general, and his own Quraysh clan specifically, since they were the direct heirs of the Abrahamic legacy.

This was a tall order when considering the fact that centuries of paganism had saturated the environment and history of the Arabs by that point. So in the early iterations of revelation, Allah revealed this *sūrah* to claim His supremacy and hegemony over the cosmos, thereby highlighting His power and might. Through this episode of revelation, He could ensure that this Message would be divinely protected despite the steep opposition of the disbelievers, while also giving people the opportunity to save themselves from Hell if they are sincere.

The Relationship with Sūrah al-Ṭāriq

At the end of Sūrah al-Ṭāriq, Allah emphasizes the gravity of His divine message for humankind, *"Verily it is a Word that is decisively final! And it is not to be taken lightly."* (*al-Ṭāriq*, 13-14) At the same time, while we find that although the divine word of the Most High is gravely serious, Allah still allows the opponents of the Prophet a respite do their worst. *"Let, then, the deniers of the truth have their will: let them have their will for a little while!"* (*al-Ṭāriq*, 17)

For the opponents of the Prophet ﷺ or those whose faith is unstable, this brief interval might give the impression that Allah is responding in a weak manner. On the one hand, the Qur'an is supposed to be decisive and final, definitively separating truth from falsehood. Yet, by allowing the deniers to have an indefinite period to freely preach their falsehood and abuse the believers, it might seem that there is an inherent problem with the message, such that Allah *needs* time to implement His Will. In fact, the truth is the very opposite: it is a sign of divine weakness if the deniers are able to dictate to Allah when and where He should manifest His will. If He wills when and where a certain event will happen, such as His retribution, nothing and no one can hasten nor delay it, regardless of whatever initiatives they take. Hence, Sūrah al-Aʿlā reminds us of Allah's exaltedness above all imperfections and His total control over the initiation, execution, and the eternal outcome of human life and guidance. Thus, He commands us to glorify His Name above all things to achieve success in this life and the Hereafter.

Thematic Explanation of the Sūrah

At the thematic level, Sūrah al-Aʿlā can be divided into three major themes. With regard to the first, Allah begins by enumerating the attributes that indicate His Lordship over us by presenting all the basic constituent forms and elements that ensure our life in this world. The mechanics of this process are simple. Allah explains the dynamics of *al-ījād* (الإيجاد), *al-iʿdād* (الإعداد), and *al-imdād* (الإمداد) in order to demonstrate that He is solely deserving of our praise and glorification.

> "Glorify in utter greatness the Name of your Lord Most High. Who has created then brought to fullest perfection. And who has disposed all things in exacting proportion then guided to its due end. And who has brought forth green pasture. Then reduced it to a blacken heap of withered bits." (*al-Aʿlā*, 1-3)

Now that Allah has firmly established the proof of His Lordship over us, we should now be convinced of our indebtedness to His infinite generosity and grace towards us. At the very least, our basic intuitions would dictate that we should wish to build a positive relationship with the One Who is sustaining our comforts in this world, especially since He has proven that He is the only One capable of bringing it to an end. Hence, through His mercy, Allah does not leave us abandoned or without guidance concerning how to build this relationship with Him; rather, He sends a Messenger with guidance to inculcate these principles in anyone who respects Allah's authority over them, and then provides a word of surety that this guidance will be protected. This in essence epitomizes the principle of *al-irshād* (الإرشاد).

> "We shall recite unto you, so you will not forget, save what Allah will. Verily He knows alike the open and yet unspoken. We will facilitate for you the Way of Ease. Therefore remind, surely reminder does benefit." (*al-Aʿlā*, 4-9)

Once guidance has been delivered, a pressing question remains: *What benefit do I gain by following it and what harm occurs to me if I reject it?*

In order for Allah's authority to be supreme and exalted, He must be able to reward those who obey Him and punish those who disobey Him. After all, laws that are bereft of any consequences can lead to injustice. If legal commandments lacked any other-worldly consequences, those who made the sacrifice to obey Him would gain no material benefit for their losses and those who disobey Him would ultimately be left unpunished for their crimes and acts of wrongdoing. In order to complete the nexus of His authority over us, Allah promises befitting rewards and punishments and gives us the free choice to decide which path to take. This is the logic ingrained within the power of *al-inʿām* (الإنعام).

> "He who fears Allah shall unfailingly heed the reminder, and he who is wretched will avoid it. The one who will avoid it shall roast in the supreme fire of Hell, wherein he will neither die nor live. Indeed, forever successful are those who reach full purity in faith and deed, and remembers to his deepest heart the Name of His Lord, and performs the prayer. But instead you all prefer the pathetic life of this world, while the final abode is far better and everlasting." (*al-Aʿlā*, 10-17)

In conclusion, Allah is well-aware that the opponents of the Messenger of Allah ﷺ claimed that he was a soothsayer or a magician and disbelieved in him on that basis. He thus reminds the Quraysh and the Jews – who were the primary reference point for the former on matters of revelation – that this message is no different than the one conveyed by their prophetic forefathers, whose legacy they claim to follow. This message of glorifying Allah, praying to Him alone, sacrificing comforts of this world for the sake of the next world, and the existence of Heaven and Hell are by no means new or innovative tenets that require scrutiny. In actual fact, they are the oldest of revelations and preached by every Prophet and Messenger that was sent on this Earth. Allah reminds these two groups (the Quraysh and the Jews) that they will find the exact same meanings in the books of the Messengers that they themselves acknowledge to be from Allah, such as the words of revelation delivered to Ibrāhīm and Mūsā عليهما السلام. And when one combines this fact with the other miracles of the Prophet Muhammad ﷺ, it leaves no doubt that the latter is indeed a Messenger dispatched by Allah, and that his Message is worthy of being followed just as the Messengers before him.

> "Verily this is in the primal pages of scripture; the Scriptures of Abraham and Moses." (*al-Aʿlā*, 18-19)

Sūrah al-Ghāshiyah

The Main Theme

With His infinite wisdom, Allah is perfectly aware that as human beings we are naturally inclined to be more certain of physical things than conceptual things. So, simply promising pleasure in Paradise without providing any concrete details is often not enough to motivate us to sacrifice some of the pleasures of this world, even if it is as small as giving away 2.5 percent of our net wealth for *zakāh* or devoting 10-15 minutes of the day for prayer. It is even more taxing and demanding to sacrifice our worldly reputations to obey Allah, because our egos cannot let go of the shallow comforts that our pride affords us when we are held in high esteem in the eyes of the disbelievers. This is one of the reasons for why Allah regularly revisits the promise of Heaven and Hell and reinforces that promise with richer details that bring our senses closer to the other-worldly plane, such that we feel that we are already there.

This is the very message that is imparted in Sūrah al-Ghāshiyah. It draws our attention to the tangible details of Heaven and Hell, and it provides us the proof we need to believe that these realities are more than merely possible. Through these divine words, we internalize the fact that they are inevitable.

The Context: Providing Perspective

When the Prophet Muhammad ﷺ began announcing the damnation of Hell and the rewards of Heaven to the Quraysh, the very notion of these other-worldly planes sounded too far-fetched to be true from their reductionist vantage point. They could hardly believe that they would be resurrected, let alone accept the concept that there was another world that was far better than the one they currently were in, or far worse for that matter. If they were to believe in the proposition of an afterlife, some of them would need to be convinced that the rewards were indeed so great that this world paled in comparison, and that the punishments were so horrifying that it would move them to see their current world in a radically different fashion. Hence, Sūrah al-Ghāshiyah was revealed and uniquely equipped to address these concerns during the early years of the Meccan period. By providing rich and sensuous details of punishments and pleasures of the afterlife and validating these realities with physical evidence, Allah is able to convince morally upright and cognizant people to think with their hearts and realize that the afterlife is the only life worth working for.

The Relationship with Sūrah al-Aʿlā

Sūrah al-Ghāshiyah flows directly and picks off from the place where Sūrah al-Aʿlā concludes. At the end of Sūrah al-Aʿlā, Allah briefly promises rewards and punishments to the believers and disbelievers respectively. With regard to the punishment, Allah said, *"The one who will avoid it shall roast in the supreme fire of Hell, wherein he will neither die nor live."* (*al-Aʿlā*, 11-13) As for the reward, Allah promised, *"Indeed, forever successful are those who reach full purity in faith and deed."* (*al-Aʿlā*, 10-14) Allah then further builds on these themes in Sūrah al-Ghāshiyah by presenting the details of what success and failure look like in the afterlife.

Thematic Explanation of the Sūrah

Allah commences this Quranic chapter by enumerating the features of the Day of Judgement with even more details than before, whereby the severity of this Day is imparted to us to the fullest extent possible. Allah only begins two *sūrahs* in the Qur'an with the opening preposition of *hal* (specifically هل), which is used to pose a question. The first occasion is found in Sūrah al-Insān, while the second instance is in this *sūrah*. This convergence is not simply a coincidence, since after all, both *sūrahs* are drawing our attention to lives beyond this current world. Upon a closer reading, we will notice that in Sūrah al-Insān, Allah is asking us about our awareness of our origin in the unseen realm of non-existence, while in Sūrah al-Ghāshiyah Allah is asking us about the news of our destiny in the unseen realm of the Day of Judgement. It is interesting to note, however, that in Sūrah al-Insān Allah is addressing every member of humanity, while in Sūrah al-Ghāshiyah, He is only addressing the Prophet Muhammad ﷺ. This is because our origins of non-existence are intuitively understood by all human beings, so Allah addresses all of humanity regarding this matter in Sūrah al-Insān. On the other hand, the details of our destiny can only be appreciated through the guidance given to the Prophet ﷺ, so Sūrah al-Ghāshiyah addresses him regarding this matter in an exclusive fashion. We need to prepare to face the details of this destiny because, depending on our level of preparation, it will either lead us to eternal Heaven or Hell.

> "Has the story reached thee of the Overwhelming (Event)? Some faces that Day will be downcast, humiliated, in hard labor, worn out, scorched by burning fire, forced to drink from a boiling hot spring. They will have no food except a foul, thorny shrub, neither nourishing nor satisfying hunger. [And] some faces will on that Day shine with bliss, well-pleased with [the fruit of] their striving, in a lofty garden. Wherein thou will hear no empty talk. Countless springs will flow therein, along with thrones raised high. Goblets placed (ready), silky cushions ranged in order, and fine carpets richly spread." (*al-Ghāshiyah*, 1-16)

After providing us ample details of what awaits humanity in Heaven and Hell, Allah knows that one might doubt the possibility of being in a place were everything is infinitely tailor-made for every whim or sensitivity we have, whether it be pleasurable or tormenting. Essentially, these doubts are grounded in a lack of understanding of Allah's abilities, for if we are evaluating the design of the afterlife purely based on what *we* can do and experience, we will fall extremely short of understanding what *Allah* can perform and create. As such, Allah addresses these doubts by giving us examples of the miraculous beings and units of creation that He has already created in our present setting, ranging from the miraculous construction of animals suited for their environment, to the divine engineering of the sky that houses us, and all the way down to the seemingly endless expanse of the ground we stand on. All these aforementioned evidences point to the infinite capabilities of the One Who can fulfil the previously-cited promises and much more.

"Do they not ever reflect on camels – how they were created; and at the sky, how it is raised high? The mountains, how they were firmly set? And the earth, how it is spread out?" (*al-Ghāshiyah*, 17-20)

In conclusion, after providing irrefutable evidence of His ability to fulfil His own promise, Allah issues a reminder to the Prophet ﷺ. He informs His loved one ﷺ that because He has created us with the free will to choose truth or falsehood, it is not within his purview or domain – nor is he inherently able – to force anyone to believe by his own sheer will or evidence. No matter how much he ﷺ loves his people and aspires to see good for all of them, it is ultimately up to them to choose to follow him, and their final judgement belongs to Allah alone. This is a form of consolation for the Prophet Muhammad ﷺ, since he is absolved of the responsibility of their rejection and consequent punishment. And it allows him to be at ease once he knows that he is accountable for fulfilling his role as a warner, and that Allah will take care of whatever remains of the affairs of creation.

"So, remind [O Prophet], for your duty is only to remind. You are not to compel them [to believe]. But whoever turns away, persisting in disbelief, Allah will punish them with the mighty punishment. Surely to Us is their return, and, verily, it is for Us to call them to account." (*al-Ghāshiyah*, 21-26)

Sūrah al-Fajr

The Main Theme

As we journey further in the second half of the 30th *juz'*, we will find that one of the main recurring themes of these short yet powerful chapters is wealth and the unhealthy relationship that many people have with it. Allah has created a plethora of provisions for us in this world to give us the opportunity to not only take care of ourselves, but to also use it as a means to attain closeness to Him and wash away our sins. As we financially invest in our afterlife and spend more for the sake of Allah, our obsession with this life decreases and our certainty in the afterlife increases. On the other hand, we will find that the opposite is also true: the less we financially invest in our afterlife, the less we will spend for the sake of Allah; in such a case, our obsession with this world will ultimately increase and our certainty in the afterlife will decrease. Furthermore, since wealth is an integral part of life, it will constitute a constant test of a person's faith. Hence, Allah dedicates *sūrahs* like al-Fajr to addressing this issue to give us clarity on what kind of relationship we should have with wealth. Sūrah al-Fajr is also instructive in this matter as it provides us examples of those who were obsessed with it and those who sacrificed it to gain favour with the Creator.

The Context: The Reality of Wealth

One of the most common misconceptions promoted by certain figures and thinkers is that material advancement and luxury is a sign of power and favour with Allah. In other words, it is common for a society to believe that if Allah has provided them a cornucopia of wealth, power, luxury, influence, or technological advancements, then He must be pleased with them, or they must be doing something morally permissible in His sight. Therefore, they feel justified to continue indulging in their rebellious exploits, feeling no need to change their sinful behaviour nor improve their relationship with Allah by following the guidance of the Prophet ﷺ that was sent to them.

Nothing could be further from the truth. If anything, an increase in wealth could be an imminent warning sign for those who are sinful, especially if Allah previously restricted their material possessions in the past and they still failed to change their ethical conduct. As Allah proclaims in Sūrah al-Anʿām, *"If only, when our disaster came on them, they had been humble! But their hearts were hardened and the Devil made all that they used to do seem fair unto them! So when they forgot the warning they had received, We opened to them the gates of all (good) things, until, in the midst of their enjoyment of Our gifts, on a sudden, We called them to account, when lo! they were plunged in despair! So the people that committed wrong were eliminated. And praise to Allah, Lord of the worlds."* (*al-Anʿām*, 43-45)

Since the Quraysh were impressed with their own social influence, affluence, and political power in the influential city of Mecca, Sūrah al-Fajr strikes a sensitive cord for those among them who invoked wealth as a benchmark of success and a measure of their self-worth. At the same time, Sūrah al-Fajr also confirms to the believers that their sacrifices for those in need and their altruistic offerings of their wealth and lives for the sake of Allah is a real sign of true success. This is because such noble actions demonstrate the contentment that they have with Allah's promise, thereby signifying that they have a spiritual richness in their heart that prepares them for all the trials of this world. They will ultimately be pleased with their Lord's account on the Day of Judgement.

The Relationship with Sūrah al-Ghāshiyah

Sūrah al-Ghāshiyah concluded with a reference to the painstaking account that humans will be subject to on the Day of Resurrection, *"Surely to Us is their return, and, verily, it is for Us to call them to account."* (*al-Ghāshiyah*, 25-26) To demonstrate the gravity of this point, Allah commences Sūrah al-Fajr by swearing on the dawn that comes after night, which is the marker for a return to life after minor death (i.e. sleep). In other words, on the Day of Judgement, Allah will resurrect us and return us for an accounting of our wealth just as He uses the dawn to instinctively wake us during the day to inspire within us the drive to pursue lawful wealth. Allah then spends the rest of the *sūrah* explaining how we should carefully and ethically account for our wealth now so that we will be pleased with our account in the afterlife.

Thematic Explanation of the Sūrah

When we read the opening *āyāt* of Sūrah al-Fajr, we should bear in mind that there are a myriad of exegetical interpretations on what Allah is referring to by 1) the dawn, 2) the ten nights, 3) the even units, and 4) the odd units. As we mentioned in our discussion on Sūrah al-Nāziʿāt, this ambiguity exists for a good reason, for Allah wants us to see the principles of these signs in the creation around us. In addition, what all the most proven interpretations of these *āyāt* have in common is the principle of worship, and particularly worship in the first ten days of Dhū al-Ḥijjah. These days are arguably the most blessed days of the year, which is in fact a view championed by a group of scholars. Moreover, these are the days in which Hajj reaches its climax point and endless rewards are accrued by the believers. If we take these facts into account, one way we can understand the import of this verse is by looking at the spectacle at the end of the Hajj season, when we see millions of people crowding at the Kaʿbah, humbly camping in Minā, and begging Allah on Mount ʿArafāt. Such individuals are sacrificing their wealth and placing their hopes in Allah's reward and blessing. This sacred display of utter neediness and an unfathomable and humble gathering of the God-fearing is simultaneously one of the greatest signs of the events on the Day of Judgement as well as a lesson on how to prepare for it. In stark contrast, the societies of the past who performed the opposite of these pious rituals by arrogantly refusing to recognize Allah's authority, stingily amassing wealth, and opposing His Prophets ﷺ became a sign of what happens to those who fail to prepare for the Last Day. The remnants of these societies can be plainly observed by anyone who seeks the reminder.

> "By the Dawn, and the Ten Nights, and the Even and the Odd, and the night when it departs! Considering all this – could there be, to anyone endowed with reason, a [more] solemn evidence of the

truth? Did you not see how your Lord dealt with ʿĀd – of the (city of) Iram with lofty pillars, the like of whom has never been reared in all the land? And with the Thamūd (people) who cut out (huge) rocks in the valley? And the Pharaoh of mighty structures? They all transgressed throughout the land, spreading much corruption, and therefore your Lord let loose upon them a scourge of suffering.Lo! thy Lord is ever watchful." (*al-Fajr*, 1-14)

Allah highlighted the monuments of these societies for a specific rhetorical purpose. This was done in order to demonstrate that these societies measured their self-worth according to the amount of wealth they *received* from Allah instead of the amount they *gave* to Allah, and by the might of their weapons instead of the power of their worship. These are blatant signs of societies who follow the same path as the haughty, materialistic, and disbelieving first nations.

"Now, whenever a human being is tested by their Lord through [His] generosity and blessings, they boast, 'My Lord has honoured me!' But when He tests them by limiting their provision, they protest, 'My Lord has humiliated me!' Absolutely not! In fact, you are not gracious to the orphan, nor do ye encourage one another to feed the poor! And you devour inheritance greedily. And you love wealth with boundless love!" (*al-Fajr*, 5-20)

The people of misguidance foolishly presume that their stinginess and hoarding of wealth will bring them a myriad of material and societal benefits. It gives them a sense of security, assuming that it will bring them comfort. But what good will that bring forth on the Day of Resurrection? How much is this temporary comfort actually worth if it results in eternal torment in the permanent realm? If one impartially uses their intellect and makes an accurate long-run forecast, they would conclude that the more valuable wealth lies in the afterlife, and that it is worth sacrificing the wealth of this life to succeed in the next. Allah urges us to internalize this fact before it is too late:

"Enough! When the earth is entirely crushed over and over, and your Lord comes with angels, rank upon rank, and Hell is brought forth face to face on that Day – this is when every person will remember. But what is the use of remembering then? They will cry, 'I wish I had sent forth [something good] for my life.' On that Day He will punish severely, like no other, and bind tightly, like no other." (*al-Fajr*, 21-26)

As for the people who gain their sense of security by exercising sincere worship and sacrificing their wealth and lives for the sake of Allah, Allah promises them that their contentment with Him will lead to eternal bliss in the Hereafter. These succeeding verses are said to have been revealed to illustrious figures of the first generation of Islam. They include Ḥamzah ibn ʿAbd al-Muṭṭalib h, who was martyred and mutilated in Uḥud, ʿUthmān ibn ʿAffān h, who bought a well and gave it to the Muslims to provide them with an independent water source (instead of making money off of it), and Khubayb ibn ʿAdī h, who was tortured and publicly crucified by the Meccans. Companions such as Ibn ʿAbbās h opined that the following *āyāt* portrayed their ultimate outcome. And this is the same outcome we too should be striving to live up to.

"To the righteous soul it will be said: 'O fully satisfied soul! Return to your Lord, well pleased and well pleasing. Join My servants, and enter My Paradise.'" (*Fajr*, 27-28)

Sūrah al-Balad

The Main Theme

When people suffer physically, financially, or socially, we usually do not understand the wisdom for such misfortunes and naturally question why such unpleasant events are occurring. In such cases, we might assume that 1) Allah is punishing us, 2) that we are too weak to protect ourselves, or 3) that there must be an enemy plotting against us. Although this typology might be partially true in certain situations, it is incomplete and fails to capture the whole story. The reason for why we feel obligated to justify our difficulties as some abnormal occurrence is because we have not yet accepted the fact that crises and adversities are an intrinsic component and reality of this worldly life. Even worse, many of us are deluded into believing that we can develop ourselves to be so strong that nothing can destroy us. The life of this world, with all the good in it, is designed to be difficult by default in order to remind us of the One Who is in ultimate control. Once we accept that, then we can start our path to understanding the inherent value of this-worldly difficulties and attain long-term benefits from them.

Sūrah al-Balad explores and brings to light this very theme. It spells in detail the nature of the life of this world, and how we were designed to live through it and accept its challenges such that we can overcome the challenges found in the afterlife.

The Context: Reframing Difficulty

The Quraysh used to spend countless hours and a myriad of resources to oppose the Prophet Muhammad ﷺ. In response, the Prophet ﷺ and his followers would spend what they could to protect him and the believers.

Noble and relatively affluent Companions such as his wife, Lady Khadījah i, and his closest Companion Abū Bakr h, would spend all they had to emancipate slaves who were being tortured for believing in the Message and to provide food and shelter to those in need, especially during the later Meccan years.

This financial struggle reached its apex during the blistering years of the infamous boycott, when all the clans of the Quraysh sacrificed their own financial relations and boycotted the clan of the Banū Hāshim and the believers, causing them to face dire economic straits and extreme hunger; this was an extremely testing period for the Prophet ﷺ, as it was when his beloved wife Lady Khadījah رضي الله عنها and his protector and uncle Abū Ṭālib died. These were the types of constant burdens that were being imposed by the leading authorities in Mecca, to such an extent that some of them would boast about how much money they were spending against the Prophet ﷺ, as referenced in the *sūrah*, *"He boasts, 'I have spent an abundance of wealth!'"* (*al-Balad*, 6)

It was within his hostile climate that Sūrah al-Balad was revealed, whereby it addressed the virtues of Mecca and the Prophet ﷺ, the nature of difficulties, and how to be successful in the midsts of trials and tribulations.

The Relationship with Sūrah al-Fajr

One of the key connections that we can draw between Sūrahs al-Balad and al-Fajr is how they both reframe our views on what will occur to us in the afterlife. On the one hand, Sūrah al-Fajr leans more toward reframing our perspective on the nature of wealth and comfort, whereas Sūrah al-Balad reframes our perspective on the nature of difficulty.

Another interesting connection is the latent nexus found between the sanctity of time and place. In Sūrah al-Fajr, Allah swears by the sanctity of time by making references to the dawn, the first ten nights of Dhū al-Ḥijjah, the odd and even days of Tashrīq at the end of Hajj, and the night, which is the most impactful time for private prayers and reciting the Qur'an. Meanwhile, in Sūrah al-Balad, Allah swears by the sanctity of specific geographic locations and people such as Mecca, the Prophet ﷺ

himself, and – according to one interpretation – the relationship between Ibrāhīm ﷺ and his son Ismāʿīl ﷺ.

What do all these concepts and elements have in common? The main theoretical observation is that all this undeniable sanctity overlaps and cascades over the Quraysh; they witnessed all the divine signs during the sacred time of Hajj, the miracles throughout history that occurred within the sacred vicinity of Mecca, and the wonders performed by the Prophet Muhammad ﷺ and the forefathers of his family tree, which extend all the way back to Ibrāhīm ﷺ. All of these signs converge together and are neatly encapsulated in the Qur'an, and between Sūrahs al-Fajr and al-Balad more than enough evidence is provided for them to submit to the truth.

Thematic Explanation of the Sūrah

In the beginning of Sūrah al-Balad, Allah exhibits the sanctity of Mecca and the Prophet ﷺ to remind the Quraysh of why they are able to enjoy the provisions of safety, security, and wealth. In a stern reminder that is not normally issued in other passages, Allah reminds them that this life is, by nature, a realm of struggles and trials. The One True God cycles people through various tribulations – whether in the form of comforts or discomforts – so they can manifest their character and prove to themselves what they truly value in this temporal world. Therefore, they should not be too overjoyed if they temporarily experience the pleasure and abundance found in this world. In fact, they should be concerned because they are under the close supervision of the Divine, and consequences in the other-worldly realm are imminent.

> "I swear by this land, this land in which thou art free to dwell. And I swear by every father and the children he begot. Indeed, We have created humankind in struggle. Does he think that none has power over him? He boasts, 'I have spent an abundance of wealth!' Does he think that no one sees him?" (*al-Fajr*, 1-7)

Oftentimes, we fall short of our duties to Allah because we are relying on own finite and feeble abilities instead of putting our trust in Allah's infinite capabilities. This shortsightedness is a primary reason for why we fail to rise above obstacles that Allah puts in front of us, regardless of whether they consist of submitting our ego to the truth, giving charity, or asking for forgiveness. This is why Allah reminds us of our own fragility in this world and how we rely solely on Him for everything, including our own five senses. Since we know that He sustains every dimension and moment of our life, we should exercise firm faith in His support when we make sacrifices for His sake, especially in the most difficult of circumstances.

> "Have We not given him two eyes, and a tongue, and two lips? Then shown him the two high roads? But he would not try to ascend the steep path. And what will make you realize what the challenging path is? It is the freeing of one's neck, or the giving of food in a day of famine. An orphan who is near, or of a needy [stranger] lying in the dust, and – above all – to be one of those who have faith and urge each other to perseverance and urge each other to compassion." (*al-Fajr*, 8-17)

In conclusion, Allah provides us His assurances that if we remain sincere and overcome our spiritual obstacles by providing charity in the hardest of times to those who need it the most and remain steadfast and compassionate, we will be handsomely recompensed in the Hereafter. Those difficulties will allow us to manifest our place with Allah in good, just as those who practice stinginess and rebelliousness will assume their place in the realm of eternal punishment. This is how we use difficulties in this life to succeed in the next.

> "These are the people of the right. And those who disbelieve Our revelations, they are the people of the left? The Fire will be sealed over them." (*al-Fajr*, 18-20)

Sūrah al-Shams

The Main Theme

We intuitively believe that when the divine truth is presented to a reasonable person, they will instinctually submit to it so long as it is presented to them in the right manner. This, however, is not how the human soul actually works. Unlike animals, Allah has provided human beings the unique ability to ignore their instincts and their intellect and instead allow their lower desires to dictate their actions and beliefs. Subordinate desires and instincts such as greed, arrogance, pride, vanity, and jealousy can drive a person to ignore the truth of Islam and even go so far as to claim that it is a lie.

On the other hand, the soul also has been provided the capacity to delay its gratification by overcoming those lowly desires and purifying them until they have a soul that only aspires to follow the truth at all costs, whereby one solely aims to please Allah and attain every heart's desire in the afterlife. Sūrah al-Shams revolves around the overarching theme that the soul possesses the free will to choose right and wrong. And it provides us a clear illustration of how far a society can go once they choose the wrong path.

Context: A Clear Example for the Quraysh

This Quranic chapter draws our attention to the people of Thamūd and highlights them as a prime example of those who allow their egos to misguide them from the truth and violate their covenant with Allah. The people of Thamūd were an ancient Arab society that predated the age of the Prophet Ibrāhīm عليه السلام. They had become extremely powerful, impressively carving their mansions and residences out of mountains, and became so arrogant and sinful that they eventually went completely astray from the message of monotheism. As such, Allah sent the Prophet Ṣāliḥ عليه السلام to call them back to the path of righteousness. They responded with arrogance and unwavering disbelief in his prophethood, and even mockingly asked Prophet Ṣāliḥ ﷺ to bring them a very specific miracle: a she-camel, full of warm milk in the winter, cool milk in the summer, and laden with meat. They further stipulated that come directly out of the face of a rock in the last stages of pregnancy.

To their utter shock and dismay, Allah granted their request and the side of the mountain split open. They then saw a supernaturally giant camel come out in the last stage of pregnancy. Quite naturally, Prophet Ṣāliḥ ﷺ then commanded them to respect the miracle that was given to them, but they still refused to believe in Allah. Instead, they resented the camel and eventually killed it. In response, Allah destroyed them and left their homes intact for generations after them to see the fate of the disbelieving nation.

This is a cautionary tale that the Quraysh knew very well, and it served as a solemn warning to those who opposed the Prophet Muhammad ﷺ and the miraculous message he presented to them. In this *sūrah*, Allah gives them a clear example of the fate of those who oppose His guidance and a promise of punishment in the afterlife for anyone who follows the path of Thamūd.

The Relationship with Sūrah al-Balad

In Sūrah al-Balad, Allah highlighted the blinding arrogance of the disbelievers by stating, *"Does he think that none has power over him? He boasts, 'I have spent an abundance of wealth! Do he think that no one sees him?'"* (*al-Balad*, 4-7) In Sūrah al-Shams, Allah builds on this topic by citing the Thamūd as an example of a people who had these very dark qualities: an abundance of wealth, the assumption that no one was watching over them when they killed the she-camel, and the arrogant view that no one had power over them.

Furthermore, Sūrah al-Shams reinforces the pivotal closing theme found in Sūrah al-Balad, *"And those who disbelieve Our revelations, they are the people of the left? The Fire will be sealed over them."* (*al-Balad*, 19-20) The former gives us a historical example of how the People of the Left treacherously behaved with a previous Prophet, and as such were destroyed by the Lord of the worlds.

Thematic Explanation of the Sūrah

This *sūrah* commences by establishing a fundamental and eye-opening precept: if we look around us and carefully investigate our surroundings, we will find that everything in our physical universe has its complementary opposites built into it. Similarly, Allah created the spiritual universe of the human soul with opposites as well, which consist of righteousness and sinfulness. We thus infer that we have a choice to decide which part of our nature to develop, with that decision ultimately determining our eternal fate.

> "By the sun and its brightness; and the moon as it follows it, and the day when it revealeth the sun, and by the Night as it conceals it; By the sky and its wondrous make, and the earth and all its expanse! By the Soul and the proportion and order Given to it; and inspired it (with conscience of) what is wrong for it and (what is) right for it. Successful indeed is the one who purifies their soul, and truly lost is he who buries it [in darkness]." (*al-Shams*, 1-10)

By now, we have become accustomed to the fact that Allah often supports His claims with tangible evidence that people can see, touch, and reflect upon. This *sūrah* is no exception to this rule. After establishing the universal principle of opposite forces in the world and demonstrating how that fundamental rule operates within the human soul, Allah then reminds us of the people of Thamūd, who maliciously buried the truth and suffered the consequences for their crimes. In the present day, we can visit their homes and see exactly how they lived and even imagine how they perished. They buried the truth in their lifeless hearts and unjustly killed the miraculous camel, so Allah reciprocated by burying them in their homes for their crimes.

> "The people of Thamūd denied the truth because of their arrogant transgression, when the most wicked man among them was deputed to kill the she-camel, although God's Messenger had told

them, 'It is a she-camel belonging to God, so let her drink [and do her no harm]!' Still they defied him and slaughtered her. So their Lord crushed them for their crime, levelling all to the ground. For none [of them] had any fear of what might befall them." (*al-Shams*, 11-15)

Sūrah al-Layl

The Main Theme

On the Day of Judgement, there will be three distinctive levels of spiritual success. The first level will be attaining the baseline level of salvation from entering Hell. The second level is being admitted into Paradise. The third level is ascending to the higher degrees and levels in Paradise.

While it is vital that we observe examples of people who have followed the path leading to Hell, it is equally important that we evaluate examples of people who have undertook the actions that lead to Paradise. Sūrah al-Layl plays a pivotal role towards this end, as it provides us the guidelines for entrance into Hell, like the previous *sūrah*, but it also gives copious details concerning the actions that lead to Paradise. More specifically, there is an emphasis on performing deeds with pure sincerity. When a person undertakes deeds without seeking a worldly reward – be it verbal recognition, wealth, or social status – they are leaving their reward to be given to them from Allah directly. This is a positive sign that Allah is favouring such a person and is facilitating their pathway to Paradise.

Whichever path a person undertakes in this world, regardless of whether it is the path to righteousness or sin, Allah will in turn make it easy for him to follow the path that he has determined. Allah will not force a person onto a path leading to Hell or Paradise, but instead He will facilitate the route that a person sincerely aspires to trek. Therefore, one must ensure that they are sincere and striving to do good if they wish to be led to Paradise, and ultimately, achieve the highest success in the afterlife.

The Context: Sincerity is Key

People usually face a dilemma when they have the opportunity to perform a righteous deed: they may either 1) choose to do it in order to purify themselves and gain rewards from Allah or they can 2) choose to do it in order to gain some favour in this world. Depending on the intention, their approach and decision might be affected and they will discriminate in the type of deed they ultimately perform.

This was something that the Companions of the Prophet ﷺ were keen about, especially when it came to giving charity. They always sought to find the best opportunity to give to Allah in a way that left the least amount of room for worldly gain or recognition. The Companions were so profound in their adherence to this spiritual dictum that it baffled the people in Mecca and confounded them. This is one of the main reasons for why Sūrah al-Layl was revealed, namely to confirm the righteousness of the Companions and assure them that they were indeed on the straight path.

One pivotal example of this peak level of religious consciousness was Abū Bakr h. He used to buy weak slaves after they accepted Islam – such as the elderly, women, and foreigners –and then free them immediately. He would spend extensive amounts of wealth in order to fulfil this task, and it became so commonplace that it baffled his own father. One day his father said to him: "Why do you not buy slaves who can defend you and stand against anyone who would want to harm you?" Abū Bakr responded: "O father, I have my own reasons for doing this. It is not my defence that I seek." As a result, the following verses were revealed about him in Sūrah al-Layl, *"As for him who giveth and is dutiful (toward Allah), and believes in the finest reward, We will facilitate for them the Way of Ease."* (*al-Layl*, 5-7)

The Relationship with Sūrah al-Shams

While the main underlying theme of Sūrah al-Shams is the internal potential of the human soul to be purified in light or buried in darkness, Sūrah al-Layl expounds upon this by demonstrating how spiritual purification and spiritual darkness are actualized in concrete practice.

This is one of the latent differences between the two themes of the *sūrahs*. Sūrah al-Shams speaks of the potential nature of the soul by stating, *"By the Soul and the proportion and order Given to it; and inspired it (with conscience of) what is wrong for it and (what is) right for it."* (*al-Shams*, 7-8) Meanwhile, Sūrah al-Layl follows this with the logical conclusion: that we will take very different paths to our destinies based on our spiritual works, *"Surely the ends you strive for are diverse."* (*al-Layl*, 4) And upon deciphering the entity that Allah swears by in Sūrah al-Layl, the difference between the two will become as clear as the distinction between night and day.

Thematic Explanation of the Sūrah

This Quranic chapter follows the same opening technique found in Sūrah al-Shams, as it points us to the daily signs around us that evidence the opposite paths that people are bound to take in this world. Moreover, we learn that we only recognize sin by its opposite, just as we recognize the night by observing the day or the male by seeing the female. The existence of opposites are essential in order for us to define and appreciate the reality of things. The paths of righteousness and sinfulness are no exception to this rule. Thus, Allah teaches us that these two paths will inevitably manifest in our lives and will reveal what our hearts conceal.

> "By the Night, when it covers with darkness; and by the Day, when it blazes forth in splendor! And by that which created male and female. Surely the striving of you all is far scattered apart!" (*al-Layl*, 1-4)

In the next section, we learn that everyone is not treated in the same manner in this world. More specifically, Allah confirms to us that our path is laid according to our relationship with wealth and how we spend it. This is owing to the fact that wealth is one of the most cherished possessions to the ego, and how we use it is a direct reflection on our faith or lack thereof in the rewards allotted in the Hereafter. Therefore, giving charity or holding it back will heavily define the path we are on, and it will become easier to reach Heaven or Hell depending on how much we are willing to spend for the sake of Allah.

> "As for him who giveth and is godfearing, and believes in the finest reward, We will facilitate for them the Way of Ease. As for him who graspingly withholds with the tight fist of greed and considers himself rich enough not to heed the Divine, and denies the finest reward, We will indeed facilitate for him the Path to Misery. Nor

> shall his wealth avail him, when he plummets fatally down to Hell. Verily, We are bound to set forth right guidance, and surely to Us belong the next world and this world." (*al-Layl*, 5-13)

In conclusion, Allah reiterates the futility of arrogance and appeals to our most basic and intuitive notions of self-preservation. The key point being reiterated here is the following: If self-preservation is the reason for why a person holds back from giving to Allah, then let that same sense of preserving one's own life and long-term interests motivate them to give to Allah to avoid eternal destruction in the afterlife. This is why Allah repeats His warning of the Hellfire yet again for those who might finally take heed to the warning after reading the previous verses with an open mind. The truth is that we will all have to face the Fire, as it will be witnessed by every human in the Hereafter. The only difference is that some people will be tormented by it thereafter, while others will successfully bypass it and enter Paradise. This is the golden rule for success: one of the greatest signs that foreshadow bypassing Hell and attaining salvation is giving up some of what you love now, so that Allah will give you all of what you love – and more – in the next life.

> "So I warn you of an unspeakably raging fire, in which none shall burn except the wretched, who deny the truth and turn utterly away. But the most godfearing shall be far removed from it, the one who freely gives his wealth, striving to reach full purity in faith and deed. Not in return for someone's favours. But seeking the pleasure of their Lord, the Most High. And soon will they attain complete satisfaction." (*al-Layl*, 14-21)

Sūrah al-Ḍuḥā

The Main Theme

Throughout most of the *sūrahs* we have discussed thus far, we have found that Allah has dedicated many of them to addressing the disbelievers and providing abundant proofs for them to believe in the true message of Islam. But it is important to note that just as the disbelievers needed regular proof to nullify their objections and misconceptions, the Prophet ﷺ and the believers also needed regular words of encouragement to build their spirits on a regular basis. Allah would often reveal *āyāt* that would lift the spirits of the believers and give them a sense of where they actually stood with Allah. Sūrah al-Ḍuḥā is one of the most elegant and comforting Quranic chapters insofar as it sheds light on Allah's relationship with the Prophet ﷺ, and teaches the believers how to positively understand their circumstances whenever they undergo adversities in life. In it, we find that Allah never abandons the believers in this temporal world of delusions. Instead, He always works in their favour, but that spiritual interest sometimes only materializes and bears fruits after trials and tribulations.

This Quranic chapter also establishes a number of other crucial points:

- The Prophet ﷺ does not decide when revelation should come down, because if he had the choice this *sūrah* would have been revealed much earlier.
- Sūrah al-Ḍuḥā also establishes that the Prophet ﷺ did not make up this revelation from his own accord. For it served no worldly benefit for him to delay his own revelation, thereby making himself look like Allah had abandoned him and demoralizing his followers during such a fragile moment of the Islamic call.
- It also demonstrates to us that worldly success does not determine one's status with Allah.
- It provides us the basis to see worldly success as a responsibility toward serving those who are in need or in dire straits, and our

ultimate success is determined by how we use the advantages Allah has allotted us, not merely for the fact that we have them.

The Context: Success Comes With Time

As a general rule, the Prophet ﷺ would receive revelation on a regular basis, and this was a means of comfort and reassurance for him. Since the early period of his prophethood in Mecca, he developed an intense love for every episode of revelation and would look forward to them as a means of gaining closeness to Allah. But when the Qur'an ceased to descend for an unusually long period of time, the Prophet ﷺ became depressed, and the disbelievers took advantage of this situation. They would find opportunities like this to hurt the Prophet ﷺ. During this cessation period, a woman from the Quraysh said to the Prophet ﷺ, "I think your demon has forsaken you." To make matters worse, without revelation, the Prophet ﷺ could not respond to his opponents with the words of Allah. As such, he had to patiently remain steadfast hoping that support would come without having any estimate of how long the interruption would last. This trial continued and caused great distress for the Prophet Muhammad ﷺ until this *sūrah* was revealed to comfort him, "*Your Lord has neither forsaken you, O Muhammad, nor is He displeased.*" (*al-Ḍuḥā*, 4) This not only crystallized the eminent status of the Prophet ﷺ in Allah's sight, but it also cemented the fact that Allah guaranteed that the Prophet ﷺ would be successful in his mission.

The Relationship with Sūrah al-Layl

Sūrah al-Layl highlights the good deeds that a person can do that will lead them to Paradise by declaring, "*As for him who giveth and is dutiful (toward Allah), and believes in the finest reward, We will facilitate for them the Way of Ease.*" (*al-Layl*, 5-7) Allah further develops this topic in Sūrah al-Ḍuḥā by showing us that we only are able to perform those good deeds as a result of effectively harnessing the blessings that Allah has given us already. This explains why Allah says in Sūrah al-Layl, "*Verily, We are bound to set forth right guidance, and surely to Us belong the next world and this world.*" (*al-Layl*, 12-13) In other words, without Allah's aid, we would never be able to be credited with the good deeds that we aspire to perform. And He proves this in a Sūrah al-Ḍuḥā by showing us how He has decreed this even for the Prophet Muhammad ﷺ himself.

Thematic Explanation of the Sūrah

Allah immediately commences this *sūrah* by nullifying the notion that the Prophet ﷺ had fallen from Allah's grace and favour. He rhetorically achieves this goal by providing us an illustration of how illumination works in the natural cycles of the world; just as the cycle of light and darkness works in this world, the cycle of revelation and silence will take its course as well; but in the case of the Prophet ﷺ, Allah provides His guarantee that His beloved's future will become increasingly brighter until it fulfils his highest desires.

> "By the Blazing Morning! And the Night when it settles darkly into place. Your Lord has neither bade you fond farewell, nor is He displeased. And certainly the later period shall be better for you than the earlier. And in time, your Lord shall grant you something with which you will be satisfied beyond measure!" (*al-Ḍuḥā*, 1-5)

In the introduction, Allah declares that the future of the Prophet ﷺ will always be better than his past, and that his favour with Him will only increase with the passage of time. Allah then ensures that this message is given serious attention by the Quraysh as well. He demonstrates the favour that He has given the Prophet ﷺ to all of his opponents by reminding them of the humble beginnings that he started from, and how Allah subsequently raised him and honoured him with the greatest title, notwithstanding all the perceived disadvantages he faced in society. Similarly, Allah will continue to raise him up as we will see in the next chapter, namely Sūrah al-Shams.

> "Did He not find you an orphan and give you shelter? Did He not find you lost and gave you guidance? Did He not find you poor and made you self-sufficient?" (*al-Ḍuḥā*, 6-8)

With the aforementioned *āyāt*, Allah has established that He has given the Prophet ﷺ the best of both worlds, which marks a perfect equilibrium in the *dīn/dunyā* binary. He has given him the highest spiritual favour of Prophethood (*nubuwwah*) in the religious sphere (*dīn*), and He has given him social status, knowledge, and financial self-sufficiency in the temporal world (*dunyā*). Thus, with this combination Allah has, in fact, favoured him above any other member of creation.

Allah then goes further to remind us that anyone who has these two advantages is obligated to share them with those who are bereft of them. This completes the favour that Allah has given us, for simply receiving a blessing is not a virtue until it is activated appropriately and is used for the betterment of humanity.

> "Therefore, do not treat the orphan with harshness. Nor repulse the beggar. And proclaim the blessings of your Lord!" (*al-Ḍuḥā*, 9-11)

Sūrah al-Sharḥ

The Main Theme, The Context, & The Relationship with Sūrah al-Ḍuḥā

This chapter is a natural extension of the this-worldly and other-worldly blessings that Allah enumerated in Sūrah al-Ḍuḥā. To present a reminder of how highly esteemed the Prophet ﷺ actually is, Allah dedicated an entire *sūrah* to further reinforce his status.

The natural extension of Sūrah al-Sharḥ from Sūrah al-Ḍuḥā is even revealed in the opening phrase of the former. When Allah lists His favours to the Prophet ﷺ in Sūrah al-Ḍuḥā, He uses a rhetorical question, saying, *"Did we not find you..."* (*al-Ḍuḥā*, 6) and in Sūrah al-Sharḥ opens with the same question, *"Did we not open your breast...?"* (*al-Sharḥ*, 1)

Furthermore, Allah ends Sūrah al-Ḍuḥā by commanding the Prophet Muhammad ﷺ to proclaim his blessings, *"And proclaim the blessings of your Lord!"* (*al-Ḍuḥā*, 9-11) Undoubtedly, the blessings of prophethood are the greatest of divine benedictions that should be proclaimed. Hence, Allah Himself proclaims these blessings on behalf of the Prophet ﷺ to eternally remind him – and as an extension his Ummah – of how lofty his status is with Allah and to make this proclamation an act of worship for us whenever we recite this *sūrah*. This divine gift even further opposes any remaining notions of Allah ever forsaking the Prophet ﷺ in this life or the next. Rather, it proves that he will forever be gaining proximity to Allah to such a high degree that it will be beyond anyone's comprehension, save for Allah Himself.

Thematic Explanation of the Sūrah

This *sūrah* can be generally divided into two parts. In the first portion, Allah enumerates the extensive blessings of prophethood that He has bestowed upon the final Messenger. These are blessings that Mūsā عليه السلام had to make *duʿā'* for when he supplicated: *"He said: 'O my Lord! Expand my breast for me, and make my affair easy to me.'"* (*Ṭā Hā*, 25-26) In another verse, he said: *"And appoint for me a helper from my family (to assist me in my burden)..."* (*Ṭā Hā*, 29). Unlike Mūsā عليه السلام, the Prophet Muhammad ﷺ was allotted these divine gifts and many more without him even being required to ask for them! Quite intuitively, it is a greater blessing to be given something without even having to ask.

> "Have We not expanded your breast for you. And removed from you your burden, that had weighed so heavily on your back? And we raised you to high renown?" (*al-Sharḥ*, 1-4)

In the second and last part of the *sūrah*, Allah explains to His creation the process through which blessings are attained. Drawing from the beginning *āyāt* of Sūrah al-Ḍuḥā, where the morning light that comes after the darkness of the night is mentioned, Allah poetically articulates the meaning of that sign by elucidating that ease and blessings come after trials as a result of faithfully persevering through difficulties. This is why the Prophet Muhammad ﷺ was given the most difficult of tests; it is because Allah gives the greatest blessings in proportion to the level of difficulties the person righteously endures. So at the end of the day, everything that the Prophet ﷺ and his true followers experience is a gift and a source of elevation from Allah, regardless of whether the decreed affair is a matter of difficulty or ease. Thus, they should find every opportunity to thank Allah and seek bountiful rewards from Him.

> "So, verily with hardship comes utter ease. Verily with hardship comes utter ease. So when you finish the day's toil, worship till tired. And seek of your Lord all you desire!" (*al-Sharḥ*, 5-8)

Sūrah al-Tīn

The Main Theme

One of the most overlooked yet greatest signs of Allah and His attributes is the human creation. Our design, abilities, and uniqueness all constitute telling evidences of a Creator Who has absolute knowledge, will, omnipotence, and of course eternal existence. Allah revealed this *sūrah* to bring these obvious yet oft-ignored facts to our attention. The more we study our own selves, the more amazed we should be at the abilities of the One Who created us. Anyone who denies such a reality is not making effective use of the intellect and natural instincts that Allah gifted them with.

The Context: From a Blessing to a Curse

An infamous example of a person who denied their own self and contingent existence was al-Walīd ibn al-Mughīrah. Allah had provided him many of the most enviable of worldly qualities, such as physical attractiveness, power, lineage, and intellect. Yet, despite all these advantages, he and others like him refused to acknowledge not only where these qualities came from, but also how easily they could be stripped away from them. Common sense would dictate that the One Who can take these qualities away is the same entity Who bestowed them in the first place.

Since these qualities were solely meant to be channels and outlets to show gratitude to Allah, their rejection of the One True God constitutes undermining their spiritual potential and thereby squandering the valuable gifts that Allah has given them. In fact, those seemingly positive qualities will turn from being a gift to being spoiled into misfortune, just as how youthful potential eventually can devolve into senility.

The Relationship with Sūrah al-Sharḥ

Unlike the disbelieving leaders of the Quraysh, the Prophet ﷺ was an example of a person who embodied all the best worldly qualities that were matched – and even exceeded – by his spiritual features. Allah demonstrates the inward and outward qualities of the Prophet ﷺ in Sūrah al-Sharḥ and Sūrah al-Ḍuḥā. Thereafter, He follows this example of perfection in Sūrah al-Tīn by showing us the faults and weaknesses of people who fail to realize their full potential: *"Indeed, We created humans in the best form. Then We abase him to the lowest of the low."* (*al-Tīn*, 4-5) Thus, once we combine the thematic value of these *sūrahs*, we attain a complete picture of the difference between what can happen to the value of people when they follow guidance as opposed to when they deny it.

Thematic Explanation of the Sūrah

The beginning of this *sūrah* can be understood in a myriad of ways. Some scholars say that Allah swears by the fig and the olive trees due to their unique qualities. Adopting this exegetical interpretation, we can view this as an analogy of the distinctiveness of the human species insofar as they supersede other animals and the rest of creation just as these two unique trees have unique qualities when compared to other trees. Other commentators and exegetes opine that Allah is using the fig and olive to represent the sacred land of Palestine and the Levant; according to the latter reading, it can be deduced that Allah is emphasizing the sanctity of the human being above all other creation when they use faith to fulfil their potential. But in both interpretations, Allah is teaching us about the value of the human being, whether in the outward form (such as the tree) or the inward element of sanctity (like the sacred lands). And just as He originally granted us a fully honourable form, He can bring us back down to something lowly and degenerate.

> "By the Fig and the Olive! And the momentous Mount of Sinai. And by this secure City. Verily, We have created Man in the best of fashions; then, we incredibly have turned him back into the lowest of all despicably low. Except those who believe and work righteous deeds – for they shall have a never ending reward." (*al-Tīn*, 1-6)

In conclusion, Allah is demonstrating two things to us. First, that He is in total control of our demise, no matter how physically strong we may have been in our peak years. And secondly, that He grants human life an eminent rank when it is illuminated with faith and righteousness. Therefore, anyone who is using common sense could conclude that the One Who has the power to humble the most powerful people into senility and death also has the ability to bring them back to life and hold them accountable for the violations that they have made against the people whom He has honoured. In other words, if He has done justice to us by creating us with perfection, then He is likewise capable of bringing forth justice to us when it comes to resurrecting us and judging our actions.

"So what thereafter could make you cry lies to the very Reckoning?
For is Allah not then the best of all Judges?" (*al-Tīn*, 7-8)

Sūrah al-ʿAlaq

Main Theme

Many of our beliefs about the world, our own selves, and the afterlife start as new ideas that remain in our heart until they crystallize into beliefs. Sometimes our beliefs can be based on false ideas that do not reflect reality (i.e. falsehood), while in other cases they are informed by ideas that reflect reality (i.e. truth). New ideas can be inspired to us directly from Allah, the ego, the soul, the Devil, Angels, or other people. Our parents are most likely to be the first teachers that introduce us to ideas about the seen and unseen worlds; such ideas usually become instant tenets, because we naturally trust them unquestionably. If parents teach a child the message of Islam through the Qur'an and the Prophetic ethos, then it will nurture the natural instincts that a child has to worship Allah and relate to the world in harmony. But if the parents introduce a child to falsehood, those harmful ideas will be automatically accepted and implemented even though they make no logical sense nor align with reality. The early years of childhood constitute a vital stage in life, such that it will likely define their religion entirely, for the Prophet ﷺ said, "No child is born except that he is upon the natural instinct. His parents make him a Jew, a Christian, or a Magian. Just as an animal delivers a child with limbs intact, do you detect any flaws?" Then, Abū Hurayrah, who was the narrator of the Hadith, recited the verse, *"The nature of Allah upon which he has set people"* (*al-Rūm*, 30).

With His perfect insight, Allah knows that most people grow up internalizing false ideas, and He recognizes that the only way to change those beliefs is by studying the truth. Reading and studying is a primary stage of worshipping Allah that never ends; this is why the Qur'an literally means "The Recitation", for it represents true ideas that are to be recited and read from the heart, thereby spreading correct beliefs as an act of worship. It also is entitled as al-Kitāb, which translates to "The Book", because it also encompasses true ideas that are to be written down to be read by the eyes as an act of worship as well. It is also called al-Dhikr, or "The Reminder", because it reminds us of primordial truths that we instinctually believe in when we compare it to the falsehood that we have been taught.

This is what Sūrah al-ʿAlaq is about. It teaches us to take the first step of worshipping Allah by reciting and learning the Book, and urges us to study the truth by evaluating our own surroundings. In other words, this book contains teachings that can be confirmed by our own independent observations which in turn lead to the conclusion that Allah is the only One worthy of worship.

The Context: The Beginning of Prophethood

The entire background story for the revelatory context of this *sūrah* has been described by ʿĀʾishah i, the wife of the Prophet ﷺ :

"The commencement of the Divine Inspiration to Allah's Prophet ﷺ was initially in the form of good, righteous, and true dreams that would occur in his sleep. He never had a dream except that it came true like bright daylight. He used to go in seclusion within the Cave of Ḥirā', where he used to worship Allah alone continuously for many days and nights. He used to take with him the journey food for that stay and then come back to his wife Khadījah to take his food like-wise again for another period to stay. This continued until suddenly the Truth descended upon him while he was in the cave of Cave of Ḥirā'. The Angel came to him in it and asked him to read. The Prophet ﷺ replied, 'I do not know how to read.' The Prophet ﷺ added, 'The Angel caught me forcefully and pressed me so hard that I could not bear it anymore. He then released me and again asked me to read, and I replied, "I do not know how to read," whereupon he caught me again and pressed me a second time till I could not bear it anymore. He then released me and asked me again to read, but again I replied, "I do not know how to read or, what shall I read?" Thereupon he caught me for the third time and pressed me and then released me and said, *"Read: In the Name of your Lord, Who has created all that exists. Has created man from a clot. Read and Your Lord is Most Generous..."* up to, *"...that which he knew not."'* (*al-ʿAlaq*, 15) Thereafter, Allah's Messenger ﷺ returned with the Inspiration, his neck muscles twitching with terror till he entered upon Khadījah and said, 'Cover me! Cover me!' They covered him till his fear was over, and then he said, 'O Khadījah, what is wrong with me?' Then he told her everything that had happened, and said, 'I fear that something may happen to me.' Khadījah said, 'Never! But instead have the glad tidings, for by Allah, Allah will never disgrace you. For you keep good relations with your kith and kin, speak the truth, help the poor and the destitute, serve your guest generously and assist the deserving, calamity afflicted people.' Khadījah then accompanied him to her cousin Waraqah ibn Nawfal ibn Asad ibn ʿAbd al-ʿUzzā ibn Quṣayy. Waraqah was the son of her paternal uncle, who during the pre-Islamic period became a Christian and used to write the Arabic writing and the Gospels in Arabic as much as Allah willed him to write. He was an old man and had lost his eyesight. Khadījah said to him, 'O my cousin! Listen to the story of your nephew.' Waraqah asked, 'O my nephew! What have you seen?' The Prophet ﷺ described whatever he had seen. Waraqah said, 'This is the same *nāmūs* (i.e., Jibrīl, the Angel who keeps the secrets) whom Allah had sent to Mūsā. I wish I were young and could live up to the time when your people would cast you out.' Allah's Messenger ﷺ asked, 'Will they cast me out?' Waraqah replied in the affirmative and said: 'Never did a man come with something similar to what you have brought save that they were treated with hostility. If I should remain alive till the day when you will be turned out then I would support you strongly.' But after a few days Waraqah died and the Divine Inspiration was also paused for a while, the Prophet ﷺ became so sad – as we have heard – that he intended on several occasions to throw himself from the tops of high mountains. But every time he went up the top of a mountain in order to throw himself down, Jibrīl would appear before him and say, 'O Muhammad! You are indeed Allah's Messenger in truth' whereupon his heart would become tranquil and he would calm down and would return home. And whenever the period of the coming of the inspiration used to become long, he would do as before.

But whenever he used to reach the top of a mountain, Jibrīl would appear before him and say to him what he had said before." (al-Bukhārī)

The Relationship with Sūrah al-Tīn

In Sūrah al-Tīn, Allah affirms that the human being was created in the best of fashions by attesting, *"Verily, We have created Man in best of fashions."* (*al-Tīn*, 4) This excellence is not only limited to the physical body, but it also culminates in the design of the human intellect and the spiritual heart that utilizes it to recognize the truth and submit to it. Without the use of the intellect, all our other faculties will be reduced to essentially animalistic impulses and only serve worldly ambitions far below the rank of honour that Allah has created us for. Therefore, in order to meet the full potential that we were designed for, we must use our intellect and study the truths that Allah established for us to purify ourselves and rise above our animalistic nature to the heights of angelic worship and awareness of Allah. If we fail to do this, then we will face a spiritual depression and become the lowest of the low, suffer in the abyss of Hell, and face the humiliation of being veiled from Allah altogether in this life and in the next. *"Then, we incredibly have turned him back into the lowest of all despicably low."* (*al-Tīn*, 5)

Accordingly, Sūrah al-ʿAlaq builds on this theme by commanding us to read and study the truth from Allah to overcome our inherent ignorance and fulfil our rightful role in creation. He also warns us of the behaviour of a person who turns back into the lowest of the low, and promises us what consequences a person who chooses that path will face.

Thematic Explanation of the Sūrah

Allah commences the first five *āyāt* of this *sūrah* by highlighting His ability to initiate creation, a process known as *al-ījād*. We should study what He says about our own origins to prove to ourselves that Allah is deserving of worship because He is the One Who created us. He establishes this by sharing with us knowledge from the partially unseen realm of the womb, which only our Creator would know. The term "partially unseen realm" is used intentionally here, since Allah knew that we would eventually develop the technology needed to see these truths for ourselves and confirm the claims He has made about our origins, which in turn will further reinforce what we already instinctually knew about Allah's attributes. Through this appeal to reflection, Allah demonstrates that if we want to know the ultimate truths of this life and the next, we must rely on Him and submit our souls to His Message.

> "Read, in the Name of your Lord Who created; created man himself from mere cell-masses clinging fast suckling at womb's wall. Read! And your Lord is the Most Generous, Who taught by the Pen, taught man what he did not know!" (*al-ʿAlaq*, 1-5)

Then Allah brings to our attention the person who refuses to use their intellect and primordial instincts in order to fulfil their animalistic desires without abiding by any divine restrictions. Even worse, some exemplars of evil will go further than this and try to stop others from worshipping their Lord and learning the truth, because they cannot bear the truth of Allah's religion being practiced in their environment at all. These are the worst of human beings; they have corrupted their relationship with their Creator and they set out to corrupt the relationship of everything around them with their Creator. Allah addresses this very example of evil and disobedience in the next section:

> "No indeed! But man will certainly transgress all bounds; merely out of seeing himself beyond need for the Divine or faith. Verily unto your Lord is the final return! Have you seen the man who prevents a servant from praying? Have you considered, if He was on the right guidance, or encourages righteousness? What if that man persists in denial and turns away? Does he not know that Allah sees all?" (*al-ʿAlaq*, 6-14)

Allah then shows us what will happen to a person who opposes the Prophet Muhammad ﷺ and takes extensive measures to silence him and his followers. It is as if we are being told that if a person does not wish to believe and declares war on the truth, Allah will destroy him and make him a moving example to others who are looking for a sign of His power.

These *āyāt* were originally revealed for wicked individuals like Abū Jahl, the archenemy of the Prophet ﷺ.

In a pivotal Hadith, Abū Hurayrah h reported: "Abū Jahl asked people whether Muhammad ﷺ placed his face on the ground and prayed in their presence. It was said to him: 'Yes.' He said: 'I swear by the idols of al-Lāt and al-ʿUzzā! If I were to see him do that, I would stomp his neck, or I would smear his face with dust.' He came to Allah's Messenger ﷺ as he was engaged in prayer and thought of stomping his neck. He approached him, but turned upon his heels and tried to repulse something with his hands. It was said to him: 'What is the matter with you?' He said: 'There is between me and him a ditch of fire, terror, and wings!' Thereupon Allah's Messenger ﷺ said: 'If he were to come near me, the Angels would have torn him to pieces.'" Abū Hurayrah رَضِيَ اللَّهُ عَنْهُ noted that shortly after this incident, Allah سُبْحَانَهُ وَتَعَالَىٰ revealed this series of verses:

> "...By no means is it thus! If he desists not, We will wrench him by his brow in blackest-grimace to his hellish fate. A hideous, lying, willfully evil brow. Then let him summon his crowd he sits with by day. We shall summon the furious hell-keeping angels! By no means shall he ever! Obey him not, but instead bow worshipfully down, and draw ever closer." (*al-ʿAlaq*, 15-19)

Sūrah al-Qadr

The Main Theme

This entire *sūrah* constitutes a vivid celebration of the Qur'an. From its descent and revelation, to the Angel that delivers it to the Prophet ﷺ, to the special night in which it was first revealed, and to the honoured personality of the Prophet Muhammad ﷺ himself, everything that is connected with the Qur'an becomes blessed. The eternal knowledge and divine speech of Allah is revealed to the creation through the Qur'an, and through that, the entirety of the world's creation has been honoured by Him. Sūrah al-Qadr brings our focus to appreciating this Message and increasing our love of Allah ﷻ through the noble effects it has on everything in the universe.

The Context: Exponential Blessings

One of the chief concerns that the Companions of the Prophet ﷺ had was comparing their deeds with the blessed works of the believing nations before them. They realized that the earlier generations of believers lived for hundreds of years, and therefore they had more time to worship Allah and increase their record of deeds. They also learned about the astounding feats and sacrifices of the believers in the past, and openly asked themselves how it was possible for them to match their accomplishments. If the Prophet Muhammad ﷺ is the greatest of the Prophets and has the best of nations, naturally one would question how his nation could surpass the deeds of the nations before him. Hence, Allah revealed Sūrah al-Qadr to manifest how blessed the nation of Prophet Muhammad ﷺ is and how their relationship with the Qur'an elevates them and provides them opportunities that no nation before them could attain.

In his canonical collection of Hadiths, Imam Mālik r narrates the following tradition: "The Messenger of Allah ﷺ was shown the lifespans of the people who had preceded him, or what Allah willed of that. And it was as if the lives of the people from his community had become too short for them to be able to do as many good actions as others before them had been able to do with their long lives, so Allah gave him Laylah al-Qadr, which is better than a thousand months." (Muwaṭṭa' Mālik)

From this point on, the Prophet ﷺ would teach the Companions j about the virtues of this night. On one occasion, the Prophet ﷺ mentioned an Israelite who carried weapons and fought for the sake of Allah for a thousand months. The Muslims were astonished to hear this, and so Allah ﷻ revealed Sūrah al-Qadr. He said: "This is better than the months in which that man carried his weapons and fought." (al-Wāḥidī)

The Relationship with Sūrah al-ʿAlaq

In Sūrah al-ʿAlaq, the opening subject of the *sūrah* is about reading and reciting the Qur'an, and Sūrah al-Qadr flows so seamlessly from this theme that Allah does not even have to mention the Qur'an by name. Instead, Allah uses the pronoun *huwa* (lit. "it") when He says, "*Surely We have revealed it on the night of Destiny,*" (*al-Qadr*, 1) indicating that He knows that the reader should still have the same Book in mind from Sūrah al-ʿAlaq.

Moreover, the greatest way that a person can honour the Qur'an and recite it as a form of worship is during the daily ritual prayers. Sūrah al-ʿAlaq alludes to this when Allah referenced, "*Have you seen the man who prevents a servant from praying?*" (*al-ʿAlaq*, 9-10) Sūrah al-Qadr further elevates the rank of this prescription by bringing to light the greatest night in which one can pray: the Night of Destiny.

Allah also asserts in Sūrah al-ʿAlaq that He "*taught man what he did not know!*" (*al-ʿAlaq*, 5). So, in the very next *sūrah*, Allah demonstrates the truth of this point by teaching us about the Night of Destiny, a blessed night that we had no idea of before the Qur'an was revealed.

Lastly, the first five *āyāt* of Sūrah al-ʿAlaq were revealed on the Night of Destiny in Ramadan. So Allah revealed an entire chapter commemorating the night in which He initiated the process of revelation to His Prophet ﷺ and commanded him to recite the divine word. Such an upshot sanctifies this night as the greatest temporal point of the year until the end of time.

Thematic Explanation of the Sūrah

Two main themes are highlighted in this *sūrah*. The primary point is to teach us how tremendous of a blessing it is for the Qur'an to be revealed in the first place. This is to the extent that everything connected to the Qur'an is also blessed, including the night it was revealed in. Allah knows that we are often oblivious to the realm of the unseen and we need knowledge of the non-empirical and non-perceivable value He has placed in different times, places, and people, so He stresses to us the importance of the Qur'an in a direct manner.

> "Surely We have revealed it on the night of Destiny. And what may teach you what is the Night of Destiny?" (*al-Qadr*, 1-2)

In the second theme, Allah provides us valuable insights concerning how He blesses the things that are closest to Him and the way that He blesses things is by surrounding them with peace, Angels, and harmony. He renders blessed things more perfect, sublime, and complete. This is what we should look for when we gauge where to find goodness and increase our value. Such a standard or benchmark is not delineated by human beings, but instead it is determined by the Creator of humanity. Allah also blesses things by instilling value in them, thereby making them more effective and productive with less work or effort. For example, Allah blessed some geographical locations – like the land of Mecca – over others by making them areas where the rewards of good deeds are increased 100,000 times greater than if they were performed in other locations. In a parallel fashion, Allah blessed some speech over others, like the letters of the Qur'an, whereby He counts 10 good deeds for reciting each letter. Or when He blessed some *duʿā's* over others, like when we send salutations on the Prophet ﷺ, and He returns those salutations back to us tenfold. The more we know where the blessings are, the more we can accelerate and attain closer proximity to Allah and become more blessed ourselves. Every sane and living being in creation intuitively knows this fact, and as such they pursue these blessings that are connected to the Qur'an. And Allah reveals these *āyāt* so that believers can pursue these blessings as well.

"The Night of Destiny is better than a thousand months! Therein the angels and the supreme angelic Spirit of life-giving revelation descend in throng after throng by leave of their Lord to set every matter that shall happen that year. Absolute peace and safety it is, to the rise of the dawn." (*al-Qadr*, 3-5)

Sūrah al-Bayyinah

The Main Theme & The Context

When people become accustomed to living lies for ages, and the truth is generally forgotten, an unspoken agreement will instinctually be made among the people to accept a significant degree of injustice and falsehood in order to maintain this abysmal way of life. This is what happened throughout history to nations that followed the Prophets of the past, such as Nūḥ, Mūsā, Sulaymān, and ʿĪsā عليهم السلام. This also unfortunately happened to the glittering legacy of Ibrāhīm عليه السلام as well. After idols were introduced to both the Kaʿbah and the rituals of Hajj, the Quraysh accepted this blatant distortion – despite knowing that it contradicted the way of their father Ibrāhīm عليه السلام – because it was financially rewarding. They also believed that removing the idols would disrupt the relationship that the other tribes had with Mecca, since many of their idols were housed there.

In order to disrupt this mass ignorance and entrenched network of lies, something significantly powerful had to appear that would bypass all the disjointed beliefs and penetrate directly into the souls and primordial conscientiousness of the Meccan community to remind them of the true and natural faith. This is how Sūrah al-Bayyinah describes the Qur'an. By forcing people to face the truth, the Qur'an made everyone who heard it question their own beliefs and reconsider their relationships with people based on one key defining principle: their acceptance of the truth. Consequently, it created deep-cutting divisions between groups and confederations who once had alliances based on falsehood. A divide slowly emerged among the Quraysh, Jews, and the Christians, because the Message addressed all their false beliefs and reminded them of the original and untainted truths of the religions that they had abandoned. Moreover, the Qur'an raised the stakes of belief by promising eternal punishment or pleasure for those who rejected or accepted it respectively. Hence, the more the Prophet ﷺ and his followers publicly recited the Qur'an, the more the frictions and tensions that emerged in a society that was saturated in ignorance. Sūrah al-Bayyinah demonstrates to us how this unfolded.

The Relationship With Sūrah al-Qadr

While Sūrah al-Qadr sheds light on the changes that occurred in the unseen world of the heavens as a result of the Qur'an being revealed to the Prophet Muhammad ﷺ, Sūrah al-Bayyinah uncovers the changes that happened to the observable realm of societies once the Prophet ﷺ shared the Qur'an with them. In other words, in Sūrah al-Qadr, Allah sets the stage for the Qur'an in the unseen realm and permeates it with blessings for everything and everyone who connects to it. By contrast, in Sūrah al-Bayyinah, Allah sets the stage for the physical and this-worldly realm in the relationships that will develop between people and the Prophet Muhammad ﷺ as a result of his mission of spreading the Qur'an, thereby revealing to us what their end results will be.

Thematic Explanation of the Sūrah

In the first part of the *sūrah*, Allah explains the nature of the Messenger of Allah ﷺ, how he constitutes living proof of the truth of the unseen realities, and how his Message entails everything we need to be morally upright in both this life and in the next. Only something as clear, persistent, and uncompromising as the Qur'an would be able to shatter the hegemony that falsehood has on society as it approaches the tremendous trials of the Last Day.

> "Those who disbelieve from the People of the Book and the idolators would never have been loosed from the binds of unbelief until the living clear Proof came to them. Namely a tremendous Messenger from Allah, who recites pristine pages undefiled; that contain solid upright scriptures providing for everything. It was not until this living Proof came to the People of the Book that they became divided." (*al-Bayyinah*, 1-4)

In the next section, Allah appeals to the basic building blocks of religious decency, which are innately recognized by every prophetic religion regardless of which Prophet they originated from. If a person intends to eternally disagree with the basic principles of the divine message that a Prophet has come with (viz. monotheism, prayer, and paying charity for the poor), then they do not really believe in the truth at all, regardless of what they call themselves. The consequences of their denial of an established and fundamental tenet should be eternal punishment. As for those among them who accept the truth and follow it because they fear their Lord more than they love their lowly desires, they will become unified in truth and reunited in the Hereafter in an eternal domain of bliss.

> "Yet they were commanded nothing but to worship Allah alone, making their religion sincerely His, holding wholly fast to pure monotheistic faith; to keep well the prayer; and to pay due alms; and that is the lasting upright all-sufficing religion. Surely those who disbelieve from among the People of the Book and the idolaters shall be in the fire of the Hell's abyss, in it to ever remain. They are the evilest of beings. Surely those who believe and do good deeds, are the best of beings. Their reward with their Lord is magnificent lush groves of Eden, beneath which rivers flow, abiding therein without end. Allah is pleased with them and they are pleased with Him! This is only for those in awe of their Lord." (*al-Bayyinah*, 4-8)

Sūrah al-Zalzalah

The Main Theme & The Context

Upon reading the 30th *juz'* of the Qur'an, we find that several *sūrahs* have referenced the accounting and terrifying ordeal that will occur on the Day of Judgement. In Sūrah al-Takwīr, Allah states: "*On that Day every human being will come to know what he has prepared for himself.*" (*al-Takwīr*, 14) In Sūrah al-Infiṭār, He further notes: "Then every soul shall know what they send ahead and left undone behind." (*al-Infiṭār*, 5) And in Sūrah al-Inshiqāq, Allah says, "*Then he who will be given his Book of deeds in his right hand, shall have a quick and easy reckoning, and he will turn to his people rejoicing! But he who will be given his book of deeds from behind his back, he shall plead ceaselessly for destruction to end him.*" (*al-Inshiqāq*, 7-11)

That said, there is still much room for speculation as to how precise this accounting process will be. What else will the Day of Judgement include and incorporate in the accountability of humans? Will it count bad deeds and good deeds equally? And from where will these records draw their information? Most people underestimate how precise the whole saga will be. Even today in our modern context, we might hear these problematic sentiments of how the reckoning may not be strict, with some people proclaiming, "Allah would not throw me in Hell just because of this small sin I committed." These questions and contentions are all addressed in Sūrah al-Zalzalah.

In this *sūrah*, Allah once again brings our focus to the theme of the Resurrection in the afterlife. But this time – just as was the case in all the previous occasions – He brings new details about the accounting that we had not considered before. Even the Companions of the Prophet Muhammad ﷺ did not know what would be included, and it was for this reason that some *āyāt* of this *sūrah* was revealed. In *Tafsīr al-Wāḥidī*, the following narration is recounted concerning this Quranic chapter:

"The last two verses of al-Zalzalah were revealed about two men. One of them deemed it unworthy to give beggars one date, a small piece of bread or one walnut, saying to himself: 'Such things are nothing. We only get rewarded when we give away something that we love.' The other man used to belittle minor sins such as small lies, backbiting, and looking at that which is unlawful, saying to himself: 'There is no onus upon me due to me engaging in this, for Allah threatens the Hellfire only against those who commit enormities.' And so Allah ﷻ revealed these two verses, encouraging people to perform even small acts of goodness, for they add up in the long run, and cautioning them against even small sins, for they will all add up in the long run."

The Relationship with Sūrah al-Bayyinah

The second half of Sūrah al-Bayyinah discusses rewards and punishments for those who believe and disbelieve in the message respectively. "*Surely those who disbelieve from among the people of the Book and the idolaters shall be in the fire of the Hell's abyss, in it to ever remain. They are the evilest of beings. Surely those who believe and do good deeds, are the best of beings. Their reward with their Lord is magnificent lush groves of Eden...*" (*al-Bayyinah*, 6-8) Building further on this theme, Allah revealed Sūrah al-Zalzalah, which outlines the principles of how this accounting will take place and some sources concerning where the information of their deeds and doings comes from. This *sūrah* constitutes a solemn warning, as it leaves us with no doubt as to what to expect on the Day of Judgement. At the same time, however, it is also a source of mercy, because it allows us to prepare for the accounting with sound knowledge.

Thematic Explanation of the Sūrah

The first half of the *sūrah* describes specific tangible events that will paradigmatically shake the foundation of the world as we know it. People will be utterly shocked to see how drastically the world has metamorphisized and rendered virtually unrecognizable. We will ultimately experience a physical transformation of the world that will cause everything that was once buried to be manifested in plain sight, such that anything that was once physically hidden to be easily found.

> "When the earth is shaken in its ultimate quaking, and when the earth throws out all its contents, and humanity cries, 'What is wrong with it?'" (*al-Zalzalah*, 1-3)

In the last half of the *sūrah*, we find that the uncovering of all the Earth's material (e.g. people, jewels, and animals) comprises a direct reflection of the immaterial revealing of information that will also be manifest by the world as well. Put in another way, we will find that the Earth did not just bury people and things, but it also kept the secrets of all the events that happened on it; it will thus reveal our actions just as clearly as it threw out all of its material contents. In fact, that related information will be extremely detailed and specific, such that every one of us will be reminded of everything that we have ever done during our respective lives.

> "On that Day she shall report whatever had happened on her, having been inspired by your Lord. That day mankind will issue forth in scattered groups to be shown their deeds. Then, whoever has done an atom's weight of good shall see it. Then, whoever has done an atom's weight of evil shall see it." (*al-Zalzalah*, 4-8)

Sūrah al-ʿĀdiyāt

The Main Theme & The Context

One of the primary reasons for why people fall into sin and commit grave mistakes in life is the error of hastiness. Haste will hinder a person from taking the time to learn the requisite knowledge that is necessary for this-worldly and other-worldly success, and will cause a person to grossly misjudge a situation. It is also a reason for why a person will end up being unable to execute a task or function with excellence.

To make matters worse, human beings are created with a natural tendency to undertake their obligations with hastiness. Even Allah says this in the Qur'an, *"Man is a creature of haste (impatience). Soon I will show you My signs, therefore, you need not be impatient."* (*al-Anbiyā'*, 37)

Nevertheless, we must understand that this natural tendency and inclination is not necessarily a negative trait. It is only negative when hastiness is attached to worldly things. But if it is directed to ends tied with the Hereafter then it can be used for good, such as performing *ṣalāh* in its early time instead of procrastinating to the later hours.

Because this is such a widespread problem that can yield devastating consequences in the afterlife, Allah revealed this *sūrah* to remind us not to be hasty with the decree of Allah and apply patience when it is necessary to gain the reward of the Hereafter. This lesson is directly addressed within the context in which this *sūrah* was revealed, as revealed in the following report:

"The Messenger of Allah ﷺ sent a military expedition to a clan of Banū Kinānah and appointed al-Mundhir ibn ʿAmr al-Anṣārī as its leader. When their news was late to come back, the hypocrites said: 'They have all been killed', and so Allah ﷻ gave news about this expedition and revealed, 'By the snorting horses...' meaning the horses of that expedition." (al-Wāḥidī)

The Relationship with Sūrah al-Zalzalah

Sūrah al-Zalzalah exclusively concentrates on the events of the Day of Resurrection and how unprepared many will be for the horrifying accounting process that will take place. This theme of being prepared for the Day of Judgement is so often repeated in the Quranic corpus that many of us forget that the Last Hour is not limited to the day we are resurrected; there is also another minor Day of Judgement, which is the day of our death.

Sūrah al-ʿĀdiyāt was revealed to remind us of the fact that death is an inevitable reality for all of us and that our burning desire and race for the material things of this world blind us from being prepared for that minor Day of Judgement, which marks the moment when most of our deeds will be sealed and stored for the Reckoning. Sūrah al-ʿĀdiyāt complements Sūrah al-Zalzalah perfectly because while the latter focuses on the reckoning in the afterlife, the former reminds us to prepare for the reckoning that will occur at the endpoint of this worldly life.

Thematic Explanation of the Sūrah

The first half of Sūrah al-ʿĀdiyāt references a breathtaking scene of horses that are charging into the enemy line. By reading the details of this scene, we realize that Allah demonstrates to us that even though horses were created to be elegant and beautiful, they are also beasts that can strike terror into the hearts of the enemy, which invokes images of an impending death. This segment of the chapter can be read to be drawing an analogy in two ways. Firstly, it can symbolize how blessings turn into a curse when we do not show gratitude for them.

Another analogy is the Day of Judgement. The scene of the horses invokes a fear of death in the heart of the enemy. The fear of death that is invoked in this scene is only a prelude to the greater fear found on the Day of Judgement, whose horrors and trials are exponentially greater. The sounds, disorientation, sparks, and feelings of surprise that are created by the horses symbolically correlates with the type of feelings and experiences that one will encounter during the Day of Resurrection. And many will be just as unprepared for it as the enemies that were caught off guard by the charging knights on horseback.

> "By the galloping, panting horses, striking sparks of fire with their hoofs, rushing to assault at dawn, stirring up clouds of dust, and penetrating into the heart of enemy lines!" (*al-ʿĀdiyāt*, 1-5)

Allah concludes the *sūrah* by teaching us two key illnesses that cause us to veer astray from the path of righteousness: hastiness and obsession with wealth. Out of His infinite mercy, Allah shares with us the antidote for curing ourselves from these illnesses: remembrance of death and the Resurrection.

> "Truly Man is to his Lord most ungrateful; and surely he himself bears witness to it, and they are truly extreme in their love of gains. Do they not know that when the contents of the graves will be spilled out, and the secrets of the hearts will be laid bare. On that day will their Lord be perfectly informed concerning them." (*al-ʿĀdiyāt*, 6-11)

Sūrah al-Qāriʿah

The Main Theme, The Context, & The Relationship with Sūrah al-ʿĀdiyāt

In many ways, Sūrah al-Qāriʿah more intensively captures the imagery and symbolism of the Day of Resurrection, whose key constituent elements have already been described by the chapters that have proceeded it. The initial shock, visual state of the people, transformation of the world, and the nature of the accounting are all enhanced and brought into sharper focus. It is one of the last *sūrahs* that exclusively describes the Day of Judgement, yet its details are so vivid that it would give you enough understanding of the Day, such that it would be sufficient to describe the Day.

The context of this *sūrah* is not based on a particular external event that occurred in the nascent Muslim community. Rather it can be based on the internal question that we may ask ourselves with respect to the ending of Sūrah al-ʿĀdiyāt. At the end of the latter, Allah says, *"Do they not know that when the contents of the graves will be spilled out, and the secrets of the hearts will be laid bare. On that day will their Lord be perfectly informed concerning them."* (*al-ʿĀdiyāt*, 9-11) Upon reading this segment, the reader might wonder, "When will that day happen?" Sūrah al-Qāriʿah directly answers this question by providing us the signs that initiate this Day. The stark reality is that even with all these descriptions and signs, we will still be woefully unprepared regardless of how sooner or later it is. This is the case as long as we do not begin to take stock of our own deeds before death comes to us.

Thematic Explanation of the Sūrah

After undertaking a comparative study, we will find that Sūrah al-Qāriʿah neatly complements the themes of Sūrah al-Zalzalah. It is as if the latter provides us the baseline number of events on the Day of Judgement, while Sūrah al-Qāriʿah builds on that foundation.

While Sūrah al-Zalzalah recounts to us the devastating earthquake and how the Earth throws out its contents and confounds the people, Sūrah al-Qāriʿah provides further imagery and details by noting how the earthquake visually affects the mountains, the movement of the people, and the overwhelming shock of the Resurrection.

> "The Striking Day. What is the Striking Day? And what will make you realize what the Striking Day is? It is that Day when people shall be like scattered moths. And the mountains will be like fluffy tufts of wool." (*al-Qāriʿah*, 1-5)

The second half of Sūrah al-Zalzalah expounds on how precise and exacting the account will be, *"Then, whoever has done an atom's weight of good shall see it. Then, whoever has done an atom's weight of evil shall see it."* (*al-Zalzalah*, 4-8) On a similar note, Sūrah al-Qāriʿah illustrates how those minute deeds will be judged: They will not only be *counted*, but more importantly, they will be *weighed* as well. And the weight of our deeds are not judged by their physical size, but the value that they hold in the sight of Allah. Hence, a person might do seemingly "small" acts of good deeds, but those actions are nevertheless heavy on the scale. Conversely, a person might think that they are only doing "small" misdeeds, but those deeds will nevertheless be heavy on the scale.

Lastly, the side of the scale that we will value the most will be the section measuring good deeds. In other words, no matter how many sins we have done, our greatest hope is that the bulk of good deeds will outweigh them. And fortunately, Allah has been merciful enough to us to give us ample opportunities to wipe away bad deeds with repentance, and also to decree for us easy deeds that weigh heavily on the scale. All we have to do in order to attain salvation is pursue His mercy with actions.

> "So as for those whose scale is heavy, they will be in a life of bliss. And as for those whose scale is light, their mother will be the abyss. And what will make you realize what that is? A scorching Fire." (*al-Qāriʿah*, 6-11)

Sūrah al-Takāthur

The Main Theme & The Context

As we learned in Sūrah al-ʿĀdiyāt, one of the primary causes of our worldly misguidance and eternal downfall is our obsession with wealth and worldly possessions. Allah reiterates this theme in the chapter which follows, namely Sūrah al-Takāthur.

Put in another way, our preoccupation with accumulating wealth distracts us from paying attention to accumulating good deeds for the next life. Unfortunately, competition in the materialistic plane of this world is a major factor in feeding our distraction. We regularly measure up how much money we make in comparison to the "average" amount others make, or draw comparisons between our living standards - which include our families and children - and other households. The more luxury and ease we see others have, the more we want to attain it for ourselves and our families.

The fatal element of distraction is directly related to the context in which Sūrah al-Takāthur was revealed. The disbelievers were so impressed by their apparent worldly advantage over other communities and the believers that they eventually died without having heeded the message of Islam. As such, Allah revealed this *sūrah* as a warning for any person who forgets how fleeting this world really is. A report related by al-Wāḥidī r supports this conclusion:

"This *sūrah* was revealed about two clans of the Quraysh: the Banū ʿAbd Manāf and the Banū Sahm. The two clans heaped abuses on each other, and this led them to count the respective chiefs and leaders of each clan in order to see which one of them had more supporters and backers. The Banū ʿAbd Manāf said: 'We have more leaders, chiefs, and members!' The Banū Sahm said the same thing. When it appeared that the Banū ʿAbd Manāf had more members, they said: 'Let us also count the dead among us.' They visited the graveyards and counted the dead, and concluded that the Banū Sahm were greater in number, for they were greater in number in the pre-Islamic period."

The same quandary actually affected the Jews when they tried to compare their apparent power to the strength of the Muslims and their competitors:

Qatādah r narrated regarding this affair: "This *sūrah* was revealed about the Jews, who said: 'We are greater in number than so-and-so, so-and-so and so-and-so', and this claim distracted them until they died misguided." (al-Wāḥidī)

The Relationship with Sūrah al-Qāriʿah

This constant pursuit of more wealth will inevitably continue until we die. But, when we finally encounter our scale and our deeds are weighed, we will find that all that worldly effort will be meaningless if it did not lead to an accumulation of deeds in the afterlife. Hence, the morbid ending of Sūrah al-Qāriʿah flows directly into the descriptions of distracted people in Sūrah al-Takāthur. We can easily appreciate this continuing theme in Sūrah al-Takāthur if we consider the following verse of Sūrah al-Qāriʿah, *"So as for those whose scale is heavy, they will be in a life of bliss. And as for those whose scale is light, their mother will be the abyss."* (*al-Qāriʿah*, 6-9) In other words, those who were obsessed with accumulating wealth in this life until they meet the grave will find their good deeds to be deficient and lacking on the scales.

Thematic Explanation of the Sūrah

In this Quranic chapter, Allah draws to our attention the different levels of certainty that can be expressed vis-à-vis the punishment of the afterlife. In the beginning, people start off with ignorance, blind to the realities of the unseen realm. And this blindness is the foundation of their obsession with the possessions of this world.

> "Competition for more [gains] distracts you, until you end up visiting the graves." (*al-Takāthur*, 1-2)

From this pivotal sequence, Allah teaches us that there are two main epistemic levels of certainty (a third level, which is outside the domain of this analysis, is not mentioned in this *sūrah*). This is one of the key reasons for why Allah repeats the same sentence twice when He says:

> "But no! You will soon come to know. Again, no! You will soon come to know." (*al-Takāthur*, 3-4)

In the next *āyāt* that follow, Allah vividly describes these two levels of certainty. The first is knowledge-based certainty, whereby we become certain of the unseen realm by receiving sufficient epistemic warrant of it and believing in it without a doubt. Everyone will eventually reach this level of certainty. But a lingering question remains: will a person reach this certainty before they die, or at the very moment of death? Those who attain it before death will have a chance to prepare for it, while those who fail to pay heed to it until the point of death will find that it is far too late. Either way, knowledge-based certainty will be just as strong as seeing an observable matter with our own eyes.

> "Nay, if you could but understand [it] with knowledge based certainty, you shall certainly see Hell Fire!" (*al-Takāthur*, 5-6)

The second level of iron-clad knowledge is visual-based certainty. This is the type of epistemic certainty that is retrieved by seeing something with one's own eyes. Every one of us will come in close proximity to the Hellfire on the Day of Judgement, such that there will be no person except that they will appreciate its existence without the slightest degree of doubt. For as Allah states: *"And every one of you will come within sight of it: this is, with your Lord, a decree that must be fulfilled."* (*Maryam*, 71) This could be what Allah is also alluding to in the end of Sūrah al-Takāthur before we will have to answer for our deeds.

> "And then you will see it with the certainty of your own eyes. Then, on that Day, you will definitely be questioned about [your worldly] pleasures." (*al-Takāthur*, 7-8)

Sūrah al-ʿAṣr

The Main Theme, The Context, & The Relationship with Sūrah al-Takāthur

While Sūrah al-Takāthur provided us the basic recipe for avoiding the pitfalls of distraction and failure in the afterlife, Sūrah al-ʿAṣr gives us the advanced recipe for success and reward in the afterlife. For instance, the notion of profit-making in the material sense – which people are preoccupied with in the narrative of Sūrah al-Takāthur – is totally reframed in Sūrah al-ʿAṣr to teach us who truly profits in this life.

We are unaware of any historical context or specific reason of revelation for this *sūrah*. Such an omission is not strange, because the best context of this Quranic chapter is our concrete experience of life itself. This *sūrah* swears by the life that we lead in this world, or more specifically, the time of our life in this world. Therefore, every one of us can use our own concrete observations and experience of life to delineate the context that this *sūrah* is addressing. Consequently, it is no surprise to find then that our lives are also a central theme of this *sūrah*. We must decide whether or not we will take advantage of this worldly life to prepare for our Hereafter; such an upshot entirely depends on our own belief and actions. This is why Imam al-Shāfiʿī r said the following golden words when referring to this *sūrah*, "Even if no other *sūrah* besides it had been revealed, it would have sufficed us."

Thematic Explanation of the Sūrah

This *sūrah* divides success into two general categories. The first category is related to our own personal development. The latter starts inwardly through the processes of faith and purifying the heart, and it eventually extends to our outward actions, which must be in accordance with the laws and wisdom that Allah has shared with us in the Qur'an and the example of the Prophet Muhammad ﷺ. Our success in this temporal world hinges on our ability to accomplish these divine ordinances within a finite timeframe. Time is rapidly running out, and we never feel that there is enough of it. The wise Muslim seizes the day and never defers his religious and spiritual commitments.

> "By time. Surely mankind is in loss, except those who believe and do good deeds..." (*al-ʿAṣr*, 1-3)

Before concluding the *sūrah*, Allah outlines to us the second category of success: developing others and allowing others to help us develop as well. Put in another way, as Muslims we are not only accountable for our own selves but we are also responsible for helping others, because Allah placed all of us in a position to be a conduit of benefit to humanity in any reasonable way possible. The benefit that we impart to others must be done with two characteristics: 1) truth and 2) patience. If we are able to maintain these qualities along with the first two, then Allah guarantees that we will indeed profit from our lives in this world and we will then reap the fruits of our noble acts on the Day of Judgement.

> "...and enjoin upon one another the keeping to truth, and enjoin upon one another patience in adversity." (*al-ʿAṣr*, 3)

Sūrah al-Humazah

The Main Theme & The Context

With His infinite knowledge, Allah is perfectly aware that our obsession with wealth is enduring, a fact which He has reiterated multiple times in this *juz'*. This is why He issues a myriad of warnings concerning the trappings of materialism and indulging in the pleasures of this world. After all, the greater a problem is, the stronger the warning needs to be.

Interestingly, Allah warns us against obsessing over wealth to the extent that He dedicated a *sūrah* to describe the warning signs and specific punishments for people who refuse to change their outlook towards it. Hence, the context of this chapter, like Sūrah al-ʿAṣr, can be based on our own experience with our relationship with wealth and the behaviours that we might exhibit as a result of the heedlessness and arrogance that appear when others warn us about it.

The Relationship with Sūrah al-ʿAṣr

The very last sentence of Sūrah al-ʿAṣr implores us to enjoin good and advise people to be virtuous alongside with the exhortation of beautiful patience. This is because, in accordance with their stubborn nature, people usually will not listen to the truth and will often be offended by it; this ultimately requires us to exhort people multiple times before they internalize the divine message and concretely change their behaviour. Moreover, in the process of giving advice, we will often come across people who are disrespectful and attempt to humiliate us in order to nullify the moral gravity of our message and incite impiety within us; this devilish counter-reaction's aim is to elicit a wrongful response and cause us to hastily react with our ego, thereby detracting us from the truth. These kind of people are exactly the category that Sūrah al-Humazah is highlighting and condemning, such that we can beware of being discouraged by their behaviour, and more importantly, becoming one of them ourselves.

Thematic Explanation of the Sūrah

In the first part of this *sūrah*, Allah provides us a terrifying description of people who are currently trekking on the path to Hell. As we already inferred from the last *āyāt* of Sūrah al-Zalzalah, Allah takes every single deed or action into account - even seemingly mundane matters such as body language. But as we will learn here, Allah brings to light the latent relationship that exists between body language and the state of one's heart. More specifically, He shows us how a person's love of wealth and the sense of security they attain from it directly correlates with the inability to submit to the truth about the afterlife and the disrespect they have with people who remind them of it.

> "Woe to every slanderer and defamer, who amasses wealth, and keeps on counting it. He thinks that his wealth will insure his status forever!" (*al-Humazah*, 1-3)

The rest of this *sūrah* is dedicated to dispelling this sense of security by giving us a harrowing description of the terrifying ordeal of the Hellfire. Essentially, every inkling of security that the wrongdoers had in this world will be destroyed and their wealth will be rendered meaningless. Their disrespect towards the truth and accumulation of wealth did nothing but increase their torment and humiliation in Hell.

> "Not at all! Such a person will certainly be tossed into the Crusher. And what will make you realize what the Crusher is? Allah's kindled Fire, which rages over the hearts, closing in upon them from every side, [tightly secured] with long braces." (*al-Humazah*, 4-9)

Sūrah al-Fīl

The Main Theme, The Context, & The Relationship with Sūrah al-Humazah

As we have seen in previous *sūrahs*, whenever Allah makes a promise or confirms the occurrence of an event in the afterlife or the unseen realm, He will follow this up with physical proofs and examples in the current temporal world. Sometimes those examples are from the natural world, while in other cases He appeals to our common sense, and in yet another set of areas He will cite verifiable events in history.

In the previous chapter, namely Sūrah al-Humazah, Allah promised a terrible end for those who accumulate wealth and obsess over their power and attain a sense of security from their worldly possessions to the point of denying the truth and denigrating the people who uphold it. In Sūrah al-Fīl, Allah follows this point with one of the most obvious examples for the Quraysh: Abrahah and his army of elephants.

This story is about a prominent general from the kingdom of Abyssinia, whose sphere of influence extended all the way to southern Arabia. His delusions of power and obsession with wealth corrupted him to such a point that he lost all respect for the Islamic legacy of Ibrāhīm عليه السلام, and even built a church to replace the Kaᶜbah as a destination for the annual Hajj. Due to his success in past wars and influence in the region, he was confident that his plans would work and ultimately allow him to increase his political power and funnel more revenue to his kingdom. This rival house of worship enraged the Arabs, who still fiercely maintained their loyalty to the Kaᶜbah, and it was said that one day an Arab traveled to the church that Abrahah had built and defecated in it to indicate his disapproval.

This act gave Abrahah a political pretext to attack Mecca and destroy the Kaᶜbah, which was possibly his original plan from the beginning. He could have set out with a normal army, but instead he wanted to show the Arabs how powerful he was in order to convert them to his newfound religion. As such, he marshalled an army of elephants and set out to storm the sacred precinct and destroy it.

However, Allah had another storm planned for him. Through His command, He deployed an army of birds that rained hellish pebbles over them and annihilated every soldier that came with Abrahah. Abrahah himself slowly deteriorated from his wound as his flesh dripped and fell off of his body until he died before reaching home.

Thematic Explanation of the Sūrah

Upon reading this *sūrah*, we learn that there are two reasons for why this story is so relevant for the Meccan milieu. The first is that the most influential leaders of Quraysh – all of whom opposed the Prophet Muhammad ﷺ – were alive when this incident occurred, and as such viewed the stunning power of Allah as eye-witnesses. They knew that their idols played no effective role in protecting the Kaʿbah, which is why Allah reminds them of how He safeguarded them before their own eyes. To make the historical context of this incident more relevant, one may consider the fact that Lady Khadījah رضي الله عنها was approximately 15 years old when Abrahah attacked the Kaʿbah. This allows us to appreciate the subtlety for why Allah says, "Have you not seen...?" when He begins this *sūrah*.

> "Have you not seen how your Lord dealt with the Army of the Elephant? Did He not make their treacherous plan go astray?" (*al-Fīl*, 1-2)

The second reason for why this story is so relevant is the fact that the Prophet ﷺ was born the exact year that this event took place, which warrants a direct connection between him and the protection of Mecca. In fact, many years after this *sūrah* was revealed and the Prophet returned from Madina and conquered Mecca, he cited this very story and reminded the Meccans of how this was a sign of his prophethood.

In a moving Hadith, Abu Hurayrah رضي الله عنه reported that when Allah سبحانه وتعالى granted His Messenger ﷺ victory over Mecca, the Messenger ﷺ stood before the people, praised and extolled Allah, and then said: "Verily

Allah held back the elephants from Mecca but allowed His Messenger and believers to conquer it, and it (this territory) was not violable to anyone before me and it was made violable to me for an hour of a day, and it shall not be violable to anyone after me..." (Muslim) Thus, this story serves as a sign for the Quraysh of the blessed nature of the Prophet ﷺ and how Allah delivered His aid and divine facilitation to him from the day of his birth all the way to the Day of Judgement.

> "Thus, He let loose upon them great swarms of flying creatures. Striking them with stones of baked clay. Leaving them like chewed up straw." (*al-Fīl*, 3-5)

Sūrah Quraysh

The Main Theme, The Context, & The Relationship with Sūrah al-Fīl

Many people are unaware of this reality, but one of Allah's worldly laws (*sunan al-kawn*) is that He sustains a disbelieving people by virtue of the believers who remain connected or committed to that particular geographical area. So long as believers reside within the contours of that society, whether at that time or in the future, Allah will usually allow that society to survive, and maybe even thrive, for the sake of the believers who will benefit from and worship in that place. This same rule of divine grace was applied to the Quraysh in Mecca. Allah explicitly says that He would not punish them due to the believing people who lived amongst them, *"But Allah would never punish them while you [O Prophet] were in their midst. Nor would He ever punish them if they prayed for forgiveness."* (*al-Anfāl*, 33) Sūrah Quraysh builds on this theme.

Mecca remained safe from disbelieving enemies since the birth of the Prophet Muhammad ﷺ. As we learned from Sūrah al-Fīl, Allah saved Mecca when the Army of the Elephants were deployed in the year that he was born. After that historic event, all the tribes of the Arabian Peninsula – and the world powers surrounding them – revered and feared Mecca and the Kaʿbah, and avoided attacking them from the fear of suffering the same fate as Abrahah. Hence, Mecca remained a safe place for the purposes of trade and worship. As a result of this security and free trade, the wealth of the Quraysh grew exponentially and their influence became unprecedented. And it is for this very reason that Sūrah Quraysh was revealed: to remind the tribes and clans of the favour that Allah bestowed upon them by virtue of the blessings found in the Kaʿbah and the birth and mission of the Prophet Muhammad ﷺ.

Thematic Explanation of the Sūrah

The first half of this *sūrah* constitutes a direct extension of the themes found in Sūrah al-Fīl. Allah is proclaiming that the destruction which befell the army of the elephant and the resulting political benefits were done so they would have the safety and security to trade northwards as far as Syria in the summer, the south all the way to the Indian Ocean in the winter, and throughout the entire Peninsula without any fear of attack. In addition, thanks to these networks and partnerships, the Quraysh were even able to build financial alliances with the major empires at that time.

> "For the security of Quraysh. Secure in their winter and summer journeys." (*Quraysh*, 1-2)

These were iron-clad historical facts that the Quraysh could not deny, so Allah cites these generous privileges and other comforts as evidence of why they should submit to the message of the Prophet Muhammad ﷺ. The chain of reasoning in this Quranic chapter is as follows: Allah is the One Who gave the Quraysh these worldly advantages; if they are so attached to the worldly comforts and obsessed with their power and wealth, then at the very least, they should follow the Message of the One Whom they know provided them with these comforts. If they cannot worship Allah out of the fear of being subjected to His punishment, then they can at the very least worship Him out of gratitude for the worldly blessings He has given them.

> "So let them worship the Lord of this House, Who provides them with food and with security against fear." (*Quraysh*, 3-4)

Sūrah al-Māʿūn

The Main Theme, The Context, & The Relationship with Sūrah Quraysh

In Sūrah Quraysh, Allah enumerated the blessings He had bestowed upon the Meccan polytheists, such as protecting them from their enemies and providing food and security to them from all the political confederations and empires that surrounded them. Yet, these blessings only emboldened the Quraysh to be in greater denial of the afterlife.

Consequently, any virtues that the Quraysh claimed to have were only self-serving, because they only upheld moral values for the sake of worldly benefit and abandoned any virtues that were altruistic. This resulted in a disturbing trend of conflicting behaviours, whereby a Meccan elite would appear generous by lavishly giving away wealth to the powerful, but would then show no concern at all for a person of low social status who was actually in dire need. Without any belief in an afterlife and final judgement for deeds committed in the temporal world, a society will eventually develop the social ills found in Quraysh-led Mecca. This is especially the case if Allah gives such a society safety and sustenance, which He mentioned He gave to the Meccan polytheists in Sūrah Quraysh.

These blatantly evil characteristics are what Sūrah al-Māʿūn came to address. While the Prophet ﷺ was in Mecca, he encountered many shocking instances of dishonourable behaviour from the Quraysh due to their lack of faith in the afterlife. It is thus no surprise to find that Allah revealed this *sūrah* to bring such depravities to their attention and as a solemn warning for any people who claim to be virtuous. In fact, the aforementioned conclusion can be directly derived from the cause of revelation of this *sūrah*:

"Abū Sufyān ibn Ḥarb was in the habit of slaughtering two camels every week. On one occasion, an orphan came to him asking him for something. Abū Sufyān responded by hitting him with a stick. And so Allah ﷻ revealed this *sūrah*." (al-Wāḥidī)

Thematic Explanation of the Sūrah

In the first half of this *sūrah*, Allah teaches us that having faith in the process of accountability in the afterlife is essential to true good character. The rejection of such a tenet is the reason for why people would feel comfortable enough to deny supporting the weak in society, as they do not fear any reprisal from a higher power.

> "Have you seen the one who denies the *dīn* (religion)? It is he who drives away the orphan. And does not encourage the feeding of the poor." (*Quraysh*, 1-3)

The second half of this *sūrah* addresses all individuals who claim to have faith, and as such can apply to both Muslims and people of other religions. After all, even the Quraysh claimed to have faith. Of course, an essential difference was the fact that their faith was in the idols carved by their forefathers, and they believed that this was a better way to serve Allah.

Regardless of what kind of faith a person claims to have, what matters most is whether that person's heart is truly connected to their real Creator. Without correct knowledge, belief, and action, a person's worship will be essentially rendered meaningless. A warning sign that one's worship is bereft of any value is that it does not encourage them to pay heed to the afterlife. Instead, they will behave only for the sake of recognition in this world because they eventually are led to believe that it is the only domain of worth and value. This is why Allah addresses the people who pray negligently in the last half of the *sūrah*.

> "So woe to the worshippers. Whose hearts are remote from their prayer. Those who want only to be seen and praised, and refuse to give even the simplest aid." (*Quraysh*, 4-7)

Sūrah al-Kawthar

The Main Theme

This *sūrah* is the shortest chapter in the Qur'an, which is not a coincidence. Allah made the theme of this Quranic chapter the abundance of blessings given to the Prophet Muhammad ﷺ in every domain and sphere of life imaginable. There is no good that Allah has given to creation that surpasses the plethora of worth and value that He has bestowed on the Prophet Muhammad ﷺ.

Abundance is not about numbers, as it is ultimately defined by the theme of quality. Something that is numerically small can be abundant in benefit, just like this very *sūrah*. This *sūrah* contains the fewest *āyāt* in it, yet it expresses more meaning than any person can articulate in three verses. Allah even challenges humanity to try and match the level of abundance embedded in this *sūrah* when He said, *"And if you are in doubt about what We have revealed to Our servant, then produce a sūrah like it and call your helpers other than Allah, if what you say is true."* (al-Baqarah, 23)

The Context

This proclamation of the abundance that was given to the Prophet ﷺ came at a time when he was still in Mecca. The Quraysh scoffed at the few followers he had, his apparent inability to save his followers from torture, and especially watching his sons dying in infancy. They cited all these aforementioned facts to mock the Prophet ﷺ and belittle his status and moral authority. As such, Allah revealed this *sūrah* as a rejoinder to the Quraysh, to reassure the Prophet ﷺ of his status, and to promise his opponents a humiliating end.

According to al-Wāḥidī, this *sūrah* was revealed concerning al-ʿĀṣ ibn Wā'il. He met the Messenger of Allah ﷺ as he was entering the Sacred Mosque while the Prophet ﷺ was exiting it. They met at the gate of Banū Sahm and started a brief conversation while the chiefs of Quraysh were sitting in the mosque. When al-ʿĀṣ entered the mosque, they asked him: "Who were you talking to?" He said: "I was talking to that man without posterity", through which he meant the Messenger of Allah ﷺ. With this statement, al-ʿĀṣ ibn Wā'il was also alluding to the fact that the son of the Prophet ﷺ – who he had from Khadījah رضي الله عنها – had died. In response, Allah ﷻ revealed this *sūrah*.

Ironically, the son of al-ʿĀṣ eventually became a loyal follower of the Prophet Muhammad ﷺ, as was the case with many of the sons of the leaders of Quraysh. Thus, by the end of his mission, the Prophet ﷺ acquired all of the sons of his opponents, and the leaders of the Quraysh were ultimately left with no one who they could pass their disbelieving legacy on to.

The Relationship with al-Māʿūn

Sūrah al-Māʿūn highlights people with the worst character and the least fortunes and bounties in this world. But Allah follows this with the opposite in Sūrah al-Kawthar by highlighting the one who has the loftiest station among all creation. In comparison with a person who *"drives away the orphan"* (*al-Māʿūn*, 2), we are shown an orphan who becomes the most generous person in humanity: the Prophet Muhammad ﷺ. Instead of a person *"whose hearts are remote from their prayer"* (*al-Māʿūn*, 5), we are provided the unparalleled example of the Prophet Muhammad ﷺ, who said, "...the coolness of my eye is in the prayer." (al-Nasāʾī)

By highlighting these competing themes in these two *sūrahs*, Allah teaches us that instead of seeking gains through hoarding wealth, undermining the righteous, opposing the truth, and abandoning worship and small acts of kindness, we should follow the example of the Prophet Muhammad ﷺ, for he has been showered with an unparalleled degree of goodness in this world and in the next. In this world he had been given the greatest miracles, the best of Companions j, the best of wives, the best of children, and the best of actions. And in the Hereafter, he will be given the highest status on the Day of Judgement as well as the greatest pleasures in Paradise. This is the very quintessence of abundance.

Thematic Explanation of the Sūrah

There are two main aspects to embracing a blessing: acknowledging its existence and showing gratitude for it. The initial *āyah* of this *sūrah* teaches us the first aspect:

"Lo! We have given you Abundance." (*al-Kawthar*, 1)

The second aspect of embracing a blessing is captured in the next *āyah*, which teaches us how to show gratitude for blessings. First, we must increase our quantity and quality of worship to Allah and increase our humility. Second, we should increase our acts of charity so that Allah will expand our rate of bestowed goodness. The more we sacrifice for others for the sake of Allah, the greater the abundance that Allah will bestow upon us.

"So pray to your Lord and sacrifice." (*al-Kawthar*, 2)

Lastly, Allah concludes this short chapter by warning us of adopting the characteristics of those who opposed the Prophet Muhammad ﷺ. No matter how much they seem to have in this world, in the end it will all prove to be worth nothing, and their efforts will lead to a total loss in every conceivable manner.

"Lo! It is your insulter who will be cut off from future good." (*al-Kawthar*, 3)

Sūrah al-Kāfirūn

The Main Theme

With respect to the fundamental matters of faith and worship, there is no middle ground. A person must totally submit to their Creator in order to be considered a believer. This means that no being can ever be worshipped other than Allah ﷾. This also means that one must believe in all the Prophets and Messengers عليهم السلام which He has named and confirmed in His Book, as disbelieving in even one of them is tantamount to disbelieving in Allah Himself. The same overarching rule applies to all the other tenets of faith, such as belief in the divine Books, the Angels, the decree, and the Last Day.

This is why Sūrah al-Kāfirūn is so important, because it leaves no room for anyone to claim that there is middle ground between belief and disbelief.

The Context

During the time that the Prophet ﷺ lived in Mecca, the Quraysh attempted to obstruct his message in various stages. They first tried to discredit his character and reliability by calling him insane, a soothsayer, and a magician. They then claimed that he himself composed the Quranic corpus of his own accord without any inspiration or revelation from the Divine. When that propaganda technique did not work, they obstructed the dissemination of his message by torturing his followers, killing some of them, and publicly tormenting others, hoping to ultimately stunt the spread of the Islamic call. Yet, such hurdles only made the believers even more firm and resilient in their faith and increased the sympathy that the general population had for the believers.

Eventually, when all of the aforementioned tactics failed, the polytheists attempted to commence negotiations with the Prophet ﷺ by offering him wealth, status, and women in an attempt to corrupt him and ultimately stop him from preaching his message. This tactic also proved to be futile, as the Prophet ﷺ refused to halt his religious mission. Such a response only manifested how sincere he was and made him even more honourable in the eyes of his followers and the general population, who were observing his rise from afar. As such, the polytheists conceived another sinister tactic, regarding which this *sūrah* was revealed to address. The details of this new technique are meticulously related in the following account:

"These verses was revealed about a group of people from the Quraysh who said to the Prophet ﷺ : 'Come follow our religion and we will follow yours. You will worship our idols for a year and then we will worship your Allah the following year. In this way, if what you have brought us is better than what we have, we would partake of it and take our share of goodness from it; and if what we have is better than what you have brought, you would partake of it and take your share of goodness from it.' He ﷺ replied, 'Allah forbids that I associate anything with Him,' and so Allah ﷻ revealed Sūrah al-Kāfirūn. The Messenger of Allah ﷺ then went to the Sacred Sanctuary, which was full of people, and recited the *sūrah* to them. It was at that very point that the disbelievers became hopeless of being able to stop him." (al-Wāḥidī)

The Relationship with Sūrah al-Kawthar

Sūrah al-Kawthar establishes the honour and rich blessings bestowed upon the Prophet Muhammad ﷺ. Allah follows that message of generosity by revealing a *sūrah* which affirms that he ﷺ must solely worship the One from Whom these blessings emanate. From these two Quranic chapters, one can derive an important connection and a pivotal lesson: the moment a believer begins looking elsewhere for their blessings, Allah will cut them off from any tangible or spiritual benefits in order to remind them of where their blessings truly come from. For, as He states in a decisive verse: *"Verily, God does not change men's condition unless they change their inner selves; and when God wills people to suffer evil [in consequence of their ingratitude], there is none who could avert it: for they have none who could protect them from Him."* (*al-Raʿd*, 11)

Hence, it is most befitting that Allah brings us this *sūrah* directly after Sūrah al-Kawthar. The former further explains the exclusive nature of our worship of Allah, which constitutes an extension of Sūrah al-Kawthar, which teaches us that the first thing we should do when we receive a blessing is to engage in worship: *"So pray to your Lord and sacrifice."* (*al-Kawthar*, 2)

Thematic Explanation of the Sūrah

Although at first sight it might appear that the *āyāt* of this *sūrah* are repetitive, upon closer examination we find that this is not actually the case.

In the first half of the chapter, Allah teaches us to draw the line between Who we worship as believers and who disbelievers worship *in the present*. In addition, Allah desires us to be clear that even if the disbelievers say they are worshipping Allah but just call Him by another name or "partially" worship Him along with others, it is logically impossible for this to be valid in any theological sense. This is because, by definition, we worship Allah – according to the divine attributes He has – without associating with Him any partners, which is not what they believe nor practice. Therefore, it is important to establish that our belief does not correspond to their definition of God, nor does their belief encompass our conception of the Divine, regardless of whether they are pagans, Jews, Christians, or any other faith. Islam and any other faith are mutually exclusive.

"Say, 'O disbelievers, I do not worship what you are worshipping. Nor are you worshipping what I am worshipping.'" (*al-Kāfirūn*, 1-3)

In the last half of Sūrah al-Kāfirūn, Allah teaches us to draw a red line between Who we worship as believers and the false deities that the disbelievers worshipped *in the past*. This is because the pagans might have falsely assumed that the Prophet ﷺ is worshipping a past idol that they no longer worship, or a false god that had been worshipped by some disbelievers from a past period. In other words, Allah is establishing in this passage that Prophet Muhammad ﷺ fully disassociates himself from any false god or deity that was worshipped by the disbelievers throughout all of human history. This distinction will continue in this life and in the next, and accordingly every person will be held accountable in accordance with the beliefs that they upheld during their time in this Earth.

> "And I am not a worshipper of what you worshipped. Nor were you ever worshippers of what I worship. To you be your faith, and to me be my faith." (*al-Kāfirūn*, 4-6)

Sūrah al-Naṣr

The Main Theme & The Context

This *sūrah* essentially constitutes a formal promise that Islam will be victorious over falsehood, and that the Prophet Muhammad ﷺ will ultimately fulfil his mission of spreading the divine message to every corner of the world. Likewise, the Quranic chapter also bids a subtle farewell to the era of the Prophet Muhammad on this Earth; the *sūrah* latently states that once his mission of reestablishing Islam is complete, he must return to Allah. Through this chapter, we are not only limited to learning from the example of the Prophet ﷺ when he is suffering from difficulties, but we also are able to follow his example when he is victorious.

This *sūrah* was revealed after the conquest of Mecca, a watershed moment where the Prophet ﷺ returned to his homeland victorious, held his blessed head humbly low in submission to Allah, and allowed the Quraysh to peacefully surrender after having caused decades of bloodshed and turmoil for the Muslims. The Prophet ﷺ had moved on to defeat the last major hostile confederation – namely the Hawāzin – in the Battle of Ḥunayn, and this symbolized one of the last major conflicts that the Muslim nation would face in the Arabian Peninsula. Once the Hawāzin were defeated after the conquest of Mecca, it had become abundantly clear to the rest of the disbelieving Arab tribes that resistance was futile, and that the Prophet Muhammad ﷺ was indeed aided by Allah as he had asserted for numerous years. Only the most stubborn of disbelievers held out longer, such as the people of Ṭā'if, whose children – many of whom were adults by this point – had stoned the Prophet ﷺ just a decade earlier.

In his work, al-Wāḥidī narrates that this *sūrah* was revealed when the Prophet ﷺ returned after hostilities had ceased in the Battle of Ḥunayn. The Prophet ﷺ would only live two more years after this conflict had ended. In this regard, Ibn ʿAbbās h narrates: "When the Messenger of Allah ﷺ returned from the Battle of Ḥunayn and Allah ﷻ revealed Sūrah al-Naṣr, he said: 'O ʿAlī ibn Abī Ṭālib! O Fāṭimah! Allah's aid and triumph has come and I have seen people entering the religion of Allah in troops. I therefore hymn the praises of my Lord and seek forgiveness of Him, for He is ever ready to show mercy.'"

The Relationship with Sūrah al-Kāfirūn

Once the Prophet ﷺ was ordered to avoid making any compromises with the Quraysh on the matters of faith and worshipping Allah, this ultimatum left only one of two outcomes. Either the Prophet would continue to preach his faith and overcome the opposition of the Quraysh, eventually overtaking Mecca and destroying the idol worship as his mission dictated, or the Quraysh would end the prophetic mission by eliminating the Prophet ﷺ and kill off his followers, since the Prophet ﷺ made it clear that he will never stop his mission so long as he is alive.

By placing Sūrah al-Naṣr directly after Sūrah al-Kāfirūn, it is as if Allah sums up the entire *longue durée* of the divinely-inspired prophetic mission by showing us the beginning of the message and the end. It serves as a strong reminder that all the fierce opposition that the Quraysh put up against the Prophet ﷺ culminated into nothing but a short interruption of what was destined to appear in the Arabian Peninsula. Furthermore, Allah establishes in Sūrah al-Naṣr that the Quraysh were so unsuccessful in their opposition that it did nothing to stop the mass waves of people entering into Islam thereafter.

Lastly, we learn that when believers are uncompromising in their faith in Allah and rely solely on Him for aid, victory no longer becomes a question of *if*, but *when*, just as the opening of Sūrah al-Naṣr begins with the temporal particle of (إِذَا) as opposed to the conditional particle of (إِنْ).

Thematic Explanation of the Sūrah

This *sūrah* is structured in a fashion that mirrors Sūrah al-Kawthar. Allah promises the Prophet Muhammad ﷺ a blessing and then teaches him to show gratitude for it. In fact, Sūrah al-Naṣr can also be considered a direct extension of Sūrah al-Kawthar, for the victory of the Prophet Muhammad ﷺ can easily be considered a portion of the abundance that was bestowed upon him in Sūrah al-Kawthar. Not only was he given a plethora of goodness in the peaceful conquest of Mecca, but he was also allotted an abundance of tribes who submitted to his message thereafter and followed him before he died. Hence, Allah says:

"When the help of Allah comes and the victory, and you see the people entering Allah's religion in multitudes..." (*al-Naṣr*, 1-2)

Once his task is over, Allah teaches him – and us by extension – to do the same thing that we are supposed to do at the end of any important task. As Imam Abū Jaʿfar ibn Zubayr r said about this *sūrah*, "When his religion was completed, his *sharīʿah* was made clear, his work was permanently established, he fulfilled his trust and message, and he knew that his life was coming to an end. Thus, a sign was given to him to signify that, namely the droves of people entering into the religion of Allah after such a long period of stalling and resistance. As such, the wisdom of Allah's *āyah* became manifest, '*...If Allah willed, He could have brought them all together to the guidance...*' (*al-Anʿām*, 35) So He instructed him to increase in seeking forgiveness, which is the same religious advice for us to uphold at the end of gatherings and at the beginning and end of the day..." (al-Biqāʿī)

Similarly, the Prophet ﷺ was told to lead us by example by showing us how to end our affairs and prepare for our reward. As the final passage of the chapter states, it is imperative for us to seek the removal of any shortcomings in our past and remain steadfast in our remembrance until we return to Him.

"So glorify your Rabb with His praises, and pray for His forgiveness: surely He is ever ready to accept repentance." (*al-Naṣr*, 3)

Sūrah al-Masad

The Main Theme, The Context, and The Relationship with Sūrah al-Naṣr

One of the inevitable results of victory is the consequent downfall of the enemy. Since Sūrah al-Naṣr epitomizes the moral triumph of the Prophet Muhammad ﷺ and his mission to guide his people, an illustration of the defeat of one of his greatest foes must also be outlined to complete the understanding of the struggle between guidance and misguidance. Not only do we learn that the enemies of the Prophet ﷺ failed in their opposition by fatally being defeated in battle, but Sūrah al-Masad also delivers a fiery warning of the eternal damnation and humiliation that awaits them in the afterlife.

In Sūrah al-Masad, we find Allah give us a vivid picture of the dreadful punishment of an uncle of the Prophet ﷺ, Abū Lahab, alongside with his wife, Umm Jamīlah. This horrifying tale of torment teaches us that no matter how close a person might biologically be to the Prophet ﷺ in this life, it will be of no avail if that individual does not submit to Allah and abide by the dictates of prophetic guidance.

This *sūrah* was revealed as a result of the initial protest of the uncle of the Prophet ﷺ,who heckled him and set an unjust precedent for the denial of all the leaders of the Quraysh after him. He was the original catalyst that sparked the opposition movement against the Prophet Muhammad ﷺ, and lent credence to the suspicions of his enemies owing to the fact that his own uncle made accusations of him being a magician or a madman.

Since he and his wife laid the foundation for the public humiliation of the Prophet ﷺ as well as directly harming him with their own hands, it is no surprise to find that Allah made him a quintessential example of anyone who follows his misguided path. The following report provides a myriad of details concerning how and when Abū Lahab expressed his hostility against the prophetic mission:

"One day, the Messenger of Allah ﷺ climbed [Mount] al-Ṣafā and shouted: 'Come to me!' And so all the Quraysh gathered around him. They said: 'What ails you?' He said: 'If I were to tell you that the enemy is going to attack you in the morning or in the evening, would you not believe me?' They said: 'Indeed, we would believe you.' He said: 'In that case, I am a warner sent to you against a tremendous chastisement.' Abū Lahab said in response: 'May you perish! Is this why you have summoned all of us here?' And so Allah ﷻ revealed al-Masad." (al-Wāḥidī)

Thematic Explanation of the Sūrah

Allah demonstrates to us in the beginning of this *sūrah* that no amount of wealth, power, or influence will be of any value if it is used to oppose the Prophet Muhammad ﷺ. Moreover, in a similar manner to previously explored chapters, we appreciate how Allah punishes a person justly, that is, according to the exact nature of their crime. So, just as Abū Lahab responded to the Prophet ﷺ and cursed him, in a reciprocal fashion Allah in turn will curse him in both this life and the next. In an ironic fashion, even the name of the flames that burn him will match his own name.

> "Irrevocably to perish are the hands of Abū Lahab, and so is he! No profit to him from all his wealth and all his gains! He shall unfailingly soon roast in a horrendous blaze furious with high flapping flames (*lahab*)!" (*al-Masad*, 1-3)

The last half of the *sūrah* highlights the punishment of his main accomplice, Umm Jamīlah, who used to aid him in his opposition and nefarious activities against the Prophet ﷺ. She maliciously orchestrated a character-smearing campaign privately against the Prophet ﷺ and used her cunning influence to encourage Abū Lahab to continue his public attacks against him. She even used to collect a pile of thorns, tie them, carry them on her back, and lay them in the path of the Prophet ﷺ so he would trip and bleed if he passed by that path during the night. These dangerous obstructions stalled the Prophet ﷺ from his prayer and preaching activities. Hence, Allah gives her special attention and includes an appropriate punishment that addresses every wicked act that she did to oppose the Prophet Muhammad ﷺ.

> "And his woman, the carrier of crackling fire wood. Clinched on her fair throat shall be a rough wood-fetcher's rope of tight wound fiber." (*al-Masad*, 4-5)

Sūrah al-Ikhlāṣ

Main Theme & The Context

If we studied the entire Qur'an, we would find that all its *āyāt* explore one of three categories: 1) the Oneness of Allah, 2) an elucidation of His laws, and 3) an account of His stories or signs. Among all the *sūrahs* of the Qur'an, only one captures all three dimensions and in terms of virtue comprises one-third of the Qur'an. That special and distinguished chapter is none other than Sūrah al-Ikhlāṣ.

The entirety of this *sūrah* focuses exclusively on providing an account of Who Allah is and what His main attributes are. Thus, anyone who fully embraces the meanings of this *sūrah* and lives according to its dictates will be protecting himself from disbelief entirely. This is what makes this *sūrah* considered an intellectual and spiritual shield from the causes and drivers of disbelief.

Many questions about God are couched in a framework of false assumptions. As a result, it can be difficult to respond to the queries of a disbeliever without first addressing the false presumptions that the questioner has already formulated with respect to Him. Allah revealed Sūrah al-Ikhlāṣ to give us a comprehensive explanation that dissects and dismantles all conceivable false frameworks in just four *āyāt*. When taken in conjunction with Sūrah al-Kāfirūn, it necessitates a complete disassociation from all forms of polytheism and removes any doubt as to Who Allah is.

These doubts and false presumptions comprise the main target of this *sūrah* and may comprise its original cause of revelation. A relevant report concerning this chapter's descent is the following: "The Prophet ﷺ was asked: 'O Messenger of Allah, tell us about the lineage of your Lord!' And so this *sūrah* (i.e. Sūrah al-Ikhlāṣ) was revealed." (al-Wāḥidī)

In another narration, a group of people posed a question concerning Allah's constitution and whether He has a body. A Hadith touching on this theme reads as follows: "A group of Jewish people went to the Prophet

ﷺ and said to him: 'Describe to us your Lord, for He has revealed His description in the Torah. Tell us: what is He made of? And to which species does He belong? Is He made of gold, copper, or silver? Does He eat and drink? Who did He inherit this world from? And to whom will He bequeath it?' And so Allah ﷻ revealed this *sūrah* (i.e. Sūrah al-Ikhlāṣ)." (al-Wāḥidī)

The Relationship with Sūrah al-Masad

After noting how Allah vividly described the imminent chastisement of Abū Lahab in Sūrah al-Masad, a reader might find it difficult to accept the fact that He would punish a relative of the Prophet Muhammad ﷺ in such a painful manner. This view stems from the notion that Allah has sentiments towards his creation and would be inherently affected by their pain, especially with regard to individuals connected to the Prophet Muhammad ﷺ. On the contrary, Allah is not inherently affected at all by anything in His creation. As such, if He willed, He could punish all of creation without any concern, or reward it in entirety without the slightest effect on His nature. Allah even said that He would bring an end to the existence of the Prophet ﷺ and punish him if he lied about any element of the revelation, *"And if he had invented false sayings concerning Us, We would certainly have seized him by the right hand, and then severed his life-artery. And not one of you could have held Us off from him."* [69:44-47] Thus, Allah dispels these false notions by following Sūrah al-Masad with Sūrah al-Ikhlāṣ, with the latter reminding us that all of us are in need of Him. He is absolutely in no need of any of us nor can anyone stand to thwart His wrath if He wills to punish us.

Thematic Explanation of the Sūrah

In the first *āyah*, Allah dissociates Himself from all of creation by establishing His existence and complete Oneness. He is One, not part of a whole (i.e. composite), nor is He made up of parts (i.e. divisible). These are the defining tenets that separate Islamic belief from all other religions that have more than one god, or one overarching god made up of smaller deities.

"Say, 'He is Allah, One.'" (*al-Ikhlāṣ*, 1)

The next *āyah* establishes his complete independence from all needs. This requires Him to be self-sustaining, endlessly powerful, living, willing, alive, and knowledgeable. Any being that has these aforementioned attributes must also be the only being that all other creation stems from. After all, in order to sustain all life the Sustainer must have a limitless power to provide.

"God the Eternal, the Uncaused Cause of All Being." (*al-Ikhlāṣ*, 2)

The next two *āyāt* are conclusions that can be logically derived from the first two verses.

This section is crucial as it nullifies polytheistic tenets such as the Christian Trinity, for in order to have children, God must have a body. But because a body consists of composite parts, this would conflict with the very first *āyah*. Hence, the third verse disassociates Him from any religion which claims that Allah has children, such as Trinitarian Christianity.

This *āyah* also refutes religions which believe that God was born from beings or entities that preceded him. For if He is the ultimate Cause of all things, then He cannot logically come from anything else, because it would conflict with the second *āyah*. In sum, the first verse is the logical basis of the first half of *āyah* 3, while *āyah* 2 is the logical basis of the second half of *āyah* 3.

"He has never had offspring, nor was He born." (*al-Ikhlāṣ*, 3]

Lastly, Allah dispels any assertion or suggestion that a thing or being can share His essential attributes. Any religion that assigns these attributes to something other than Allah is worshipping a false God. For if we establish the last three *āyāt*, they completely nullify believing in more than one god, a god that precedes Allah, or a god that comes from Allah. Believing in any one of these three claims would lead to an absurd upshot. If there was a god that existed distinctly or separately from Allah, one of them would have to be false, because a Being with absolute will, by definition, can only exist when there is nothing that has the power to restrict it. And as Allah proves throughout the Quranic corpus, nothing can restrict Him from doing what He wants.

"And there is none comparable to Him." (*al-Ikhlāṣ*, 4)

Sūrahs al-Falaq & al-Nās

The Main Theme, The Context, & The Relationship with Sūrah al-Ikhlāṣ

When we read Sūrah al-Fātiḥah in the beginning of the Qur'an, we find that Allah orders us to ask Him for guidance, *"Guide us on the straight path."* (*al-Fātiḥah*, 5) Interestingly, it can be said that the rest of the Qur'an teaches us everything we need to know about that Path and how to attain Allah's acceptance. However, just like in the case of our father Adam ﷺ, we come to the realization that simply knowing the path is not sufficient to achieving success, and that we must also protect ourselves from the means of misguidance and trappings that our enemies employ to lead us away from Allah.

Therefore, in the end of the Qur'an, Allah provides us the most powerful words of divine protection that we can invoke to shield us from all forms of evil. These chapters are so powerful that they are colloquially known as "The Three Quls". They consist of the following chapters: 1) Sūrah al-Ikhlāṣ, 2) Sūrah al-Falaq, and 3) Sūrah al-Nās.

Sūrah al-Ikhlāṣ arms us with a fortified understanding of Who Allah is, which shields us from all arguments that cast doubts or confusion about the nature of Allah in our hearts. By fully embracing and internalizing the meanings of this *sūrah* and reciting it often, we will remove all forms of polytheism and idolatry from our minds, and purify our hearts from doubting and misunderstanding Allah's attributes. Once belief in this noble chapter extends its roots in the soul, it will become an impenetrable shield against all theological attacks from the opponents of the Message. The more we develop an appreciation and love for this *sūrah*, the closer we will draw to Paradise. Anas ibn Mālik h reported: "A man said, 'O Messenger of Allah, I love this chapter: *"Say: He is Allah, the One"*'" (*al-Ikhlāṣ*, 1). The Messenger of Allah ﷺ said, *'Your love for it will admit you into Paradise.'*" (al-Bukhārī)

Once Allah has provided us protection from disbelief, He further increases His blessing by thwarting the physical harms of our enemies through the divine mechanism of Sūrah al-Falaq. This *sūrah* protects us from all forms of worldly evil, whether physical or metaphysical. They include the evil arts, such as the harmful effects of magic, the evil eye, plots of jealousy, and the devilish harms and dangers that are registered by the different forms of creation.

Lastly, after protecting our faith and our bodies, Allah completes His favour by teaching us Sūrah al-Nās, which safeguards our spirits from the internal afflictions that come from the evil whispers of devils. Taken as a cohesive whole, all three of these *sūrahs* ensure the protection of our minds, hearts, and bodies. This is why Allah revealed these last two *sūrahs* when the Prophet ﷺ was afflicted with magic. Even after he recovered, he continued to recite these *sūrahs* for the purpose of attaining Allah's protection every day and night.

Lady ʿĀ'ishah رضي الله عنها narrates in an authentic Hadith: "Whenever the Prophet ﷺ went to bed every night, he used to cup his hands together and blow over them after reciting Sūrah al-Ikhlāṣ, Sūrah al-Falaq, and Sūrah al-Nās. He would then rub his hands over whatever parts of his body he was able to rub, starting with his head, face, and front of the body. He used to do that three times." (al-Bukhārī)

Thematic Explanation of the Sūrah

Sūrah al-Falaq commences by teaching us that there is always an inherent wisdom and goodness that comes with things that may appear to be wrong or immoral. In His infinite knowledge, Allah created darkness for a wise purpose, and He allowed jealousy and magic to happen for a wise purpose. As a result, we cannot expect the total eradication of such maladies and wrongs. Rather, we can hope for being protected from their *harm* while benefiting from their indirect advantages.

While it might seem counterintuitive for a victim, there are actually a myriad of indirect advantages to harmful things and harmful people. For one thing, on some occasions Allah allows oppressors to subdue other oppressors as a form of retribution for their sins. For He says in a powerful verse, *"Thus do We make the oppressors have power over each other because of what they earn."* (*al-An'ām*, 169) Paradoxically, oppressors and malevolent people actually do harm to themselves during the process of attempting to harm others, and this is one of the reasons for why Allah allowed enemies like Fir'awn to execute his schemes and plots. Allah will use their own schemes against themselves while purifying the believers and raising their ranks in the Hereafter.

Hence, Allah teaches us to invoke His power to bring goodness and blessings out of dreadful situations just as He brings light out of the darkness.

> "Say: I take refuge in the Lord of Daybreak; from the evil of all He has created. And from the evil of outpoured blackest night when it fills everything. And from the evil of wicked souls who blow spittle mist on sorcerous knots. And from the evil of an envier, when gripped by envy." (*al-Falaq*, 1-5)

Since the last episode of evil mentioned in Sūrah al-Falaq is related to the ego (i.e. the envier), Allah dedicates the entire final chapter to protecting ourselves from the harms associated with the ego. In Sūrah al-Falaq, Allah informs us to invoke Him in one manner, while in Sūrah al-Nās He advises us to invoke Him in three ways. This should indicate to us how much more complex and difficult it is to protect one's self from the types of harm alluded in Sūrah al-Nās. It also teaches us that the harm that emanates from our own selves – which is highlighted in Sūrah al-Nās – is far worse than the harm that emanates from others, as highlighted in al-Falaq.

> "Say: I take refuge from the Lord of Men, the King of Men, the God of Men; from the evil of the withdrawing insinuator of ill-thoughts." (*al-Nās*, 1-4)

The last *āyah* highlights the fact that all evil thoughts emanate from either the Devil or the impure ego. Both of them reside inside of us and constantly inspire us to fall into sin, to indulge in immoral thoughts, and to speak sinfully. Reciting the Qur'an, especially these three *sūrahs*, subdues these voices within us and repels the Devil from our bodies, thereby allowing virtuous, moral, and pure thoughts to prevail.

"...Who sows and sows ill-thoughts in the breasts of men; be he of vile *jinn* or men." (*al-Nās*, 5-6)

In conclusion, once virtuous thoughts become predominant within our souls, we will be inspired to undertake morally upright and praiseworthy actions, which in turn will place us us on the straight path of guidance. Without Allah's help, we would certainly be lost and trekking the path of disobedience and evil. Therefore, after finishing the Qur'an we return back to Allah with the hopes that He will facilitate to us the path of guidance. We thus recite Sūrah al-Fātiḥah once more, hoping to remain on the straight path until our last breath, unconditionally remaining grateful to Allah everyday by saying, "*...All praise belongs to Allah, Lord of the Worlds.*" (*al-Fātiḥah*, 1)

This Ends Volume One.

www.ingramcontent.com/pod-product-compliance
Lightning Source LLC
Chambersburg PA
CBHW020201090426
42734CB00008B/900
* 9 7 8 1 9 6 6 3 2 9 8 8 6 *